GLENCOE

The American Journey

Early Years

IN GRAPHIC NOVEL

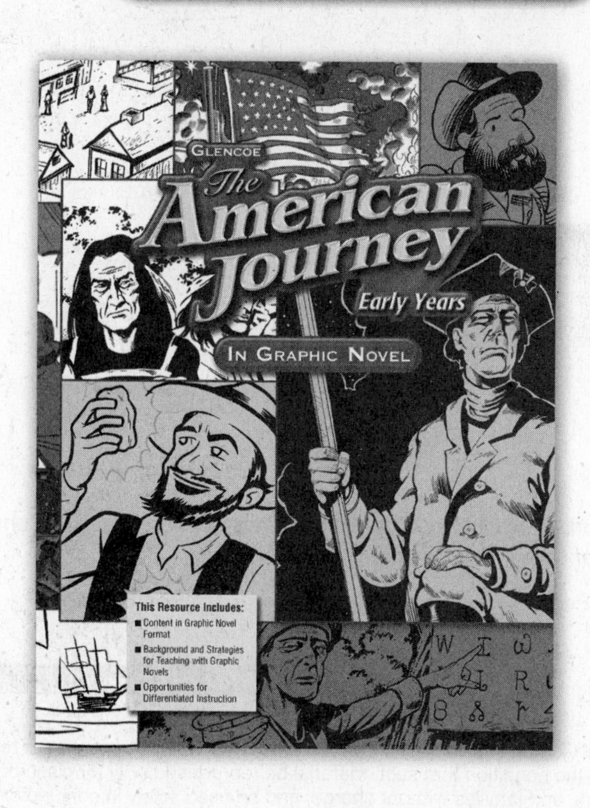

Illustrators: *Shane McDermott, Ellen Lindner, Joel Priddy, Greg Lawhun, Mitch O'Connell, Mark Carolan, John Pham, Pat Lewis, Brian Ralph, Gregory Benton*

The McGraw·Hill Companies

Send all inquiries to:

Glencoe/McGraw-Hill
8787 Orion Place
Columbus, OH 43240-4027

ISBN: 978-0-07-880674-2
MHID: 0-07-880674-7

Printed in the United States of America.

1 2 3 4 5 6 066 12 11 10 09 08

TABLE OF CONTENTS

USING GRAPHIC NOVELS:
POPULAR CULTURE AND SOCIAL STUDIES INTERACT

Graphic novels represent a significant segment of the literary market for adolescents and young adults. These stories may resemble comic books, but on closer inspection, they often address controversial issues using complex story lines. Some graphic novels that are well known to Western audiences are *Watchmen,* which examines how superheroes live in a society that has turned against them; *Maus,* which uses anthropomorphic characters to tell the story of a Holocaust survivor; and *From Hell,* which presents one explanation for the actions of the historical serial killer Jack the Ripper.

WHAT ARE GRAPHIC NOVELS?

Graphic novels, as they are known in Western countries, were initially inspired by Japanese *manga* (comics) and *anime* (animation). *Anime* style is most commonly recognizable in its use of large-eyed characters with oversized heads, and it has increasingly been recognized by Western audiences as a distinct art form.

Use of the *manga* genre in Japan is far more widespread than in Western countries and dates back to the early part of the 1900s. Japanese *manga,* rendered in black and white and printed on newsprint, are read by children and adults and include many topics, although science fiction *mechas* (robots) dominate the field. The topics of these works are surprisingly similar to Western young adult fiction. A large portion of the market is *shojo,* comic books designed to appeal to girls. A popular *shojo* character that appears in America is the *Sailor Moon* series, featuring a resourceful Japanese schoolgirl. *Shonen manga* is designed primarily for boys and usually consists of action stories. Teachers may recognize elements of *shonen manga* in Japanese game cards collected and traded by many American youth. Many *manga* are published in serial form in books as long as 750 pages. One of the first *manga* marketed for Western consumption was *The Four Immigrants Manga: A Japanese Experience in San Francisco, 1904–1924* (Kiyama, 1999), first published in 1931. It is not in the *anime* style of today's novels, but offers a poignant portrayal of the challenges facing Asian immigrants at the time.

Why Do Graphic Novels Appeal to Students?

Part of the appeal of graphic novels lies in their "underground" (and therefore forbidden) reputation. Another part of the appeal of *manga* and *anime* lies in their sophisticated story lines and the development of complex characters (Izawa, 2002). Unlike American comic books that feature a superhero with fixed and exaggerated attributes, many of these Japanese stories include a subtext of universal themes involving ethical and moral dilemmas. These *gekiga* (literary novels) are ambitious in their scope and intricacy and are becoming more available in English translations. Unlike the broad range of stories available in Japan, however, the stream of *manga* and *anime* reaching Western readers is not so diverse. The bulk of *manga* and *anime* available in America are often skewed toward violent and sexually graphic titles (called *hentai,* or "perverse") which do not reflect the wide range of quality available.

Graphic novels continue to develop and diversify (Frey & Fisher, 2004). Interactive graphic novels presented in serial form are appearing on the Internet. Readers have a number of options when they visit the site each month to view the next installment, such as engaging in role-playing games, creating new characters to interact with those developed by the author, and visiting an extensive catalog for background information. Most of these Web-based graphic novels have decidedly adult content, although users are likely to be Web-savvy adolescents. A unique subset of these graphic novels and *manga* is a style of writing called *fanfiction,* in which readers create and post their own alternative versions of stories featuring their favorite characters (e.g., Chandler-Olcott & Mahar, 2003).

Why Use Graphic Novels in Social Studies?

Graphic novels are amazingly diverse, in terms of both their content and their usefulness. For example, Gorman (2002) notes that graphic novels are exactly what teens are looking for: they are motivating, engaging, challenging, and interesting. Schwartz (2002b, 2004) believes that graphic novels are engaging because they allow teachers to enter the youth culture and students to bring their "out of school" experiences into the classroom. The purpose of such **"multiple literacies,"** is to bridge the gap between students' school literacy and the ways in which they use reading and writing outside of school.

Graphic novels have also been used effectively with students with disabilities, students who struggle with reading, and English language learners (e.g., Cary, 2004; Frey & Fisher, 2004; Schwartz, 2002a). One of the theories behind the use of graphic novels for struggling adolescent readers focuses on their effectiveness in presenting complex ideas while reducing the reading demands. As a result, all students can thoughtfully discuss the content at hand. As Weiner (2003) noted,

> Graphic novels have found their way into the classroom, as teachers are realizing their usefulness as literacy tools. After a study of graphic novels, researchers concluded that the average graphic novel introduced readers to twice as many words as the average children's book. This realization has reinforced the idea that the comics format is a good way to impart information. (p. 61)

Conclusions

While controversy about graphic novels persists—especially among people who worry that graphic novels will bring the end of traditional books—our experiences with adolescents, as well as a number of current research studies, suggest that graphic novels are an important adjunct in our instruction. Graphic novels are viable options for students with disabilities, struggling readers, and English language learners, but they are more powerful than that. Graphic novels are motivating and engaging for all students. They allow us to differentiate our instruction and provide universal access to the curriculum. We hope you'll find the graphic novels in this book useful, as you engage your students in the study of history and social studies.

Sincerely,

Douglas Fisher & Nancy Frey

Douglas Fisher, Ph.D.
Professor
San Diego State University

Nancy Frey, Ph.D.
Assistant Professor
San Diego State University

References

Cary, S. (2004) Going graphic: *Comics at work in the multilingual classroom.* Portsmouth, NH: Heinemann.

Chandler-Olcott, K., & Mahar, D. (2003). Adolescents' anime-inspired "fanfictions": An exploration of multiliteracies. *Journal of Adolescent & Adult Literacy,* 46, 556–566.

Fisher, D., & Frey, N. (2004). *Improving adolescent literacy: Strategies at work.* Upper Saddle River, NJ: Merrill Education.

Frey, N., & Fisher, D. (2004). Using graphic novels, anime, and the Internet in an urban high school. *English Journal, 93*(3), 19–25.

Gorman, M. (2002). What teens want: Thirty graphic novels you can't live without. *School Library Journal, 48*(8) 42–47.

Izawa, E. (2004). *What are manga and anime?* Retrieved December 5, 2004, from www.mit.edu:8001/people/rei/Expl.html.

Kiyama, H. Y. (1999). *The four immigrants manga: A Japanese experience in San Francisco, 1904–1924.* Berkeley, CA: Stone Bridge Press.

Schwarz, G. (2002a). Graphic books for diverse needs: Engaging reluctant and curious readers. *ALAN Review, 30*(1), 54–57.

Schwarz, G. E. (2002b). Graphic novels for multiple literacies. *Journal of Adolescent & Adult Literacy, 46,* 262–265.

Schwarz, G. E. (2004). Graphic novels: Multiple cultures and multiple literacies. *Thinking Classroom, 5*(4), 17–24.

Weiner, S. (2003). *The rise of the graphic novel: Faster than a speeding bullet.* New York: Nantier Beall Minoustchine Publishing.

Teaching Strategies for Graphic Novels

As we have noted, graphic novels are an excellent adjunct text. While they cannot and should not replace reading or the core, standards-based textbook, they can be used effectively to build students' background knowledge, to motivate students, to provide a different access route to the content, and to allow students to check and review their work.

Strategies for using graphic novels in the classroom include the following:

1. **Previewing Content.** In advance of the text reading, you can use a graphic novel as a way to activate background information and prior knowledge. For example, you may display a graphic novel on the overhead projector and discuss it with the class. Using a teacher think-aloud, in which you share your thinking about the graphic novel with the class, you might provide students with advance information that they will read later in the book. Alternatively, you may display the graphic novel and invite students, in pairs or groups, to share their thinking with one another. Regardless of the approach, the goal is to activate students' interest and background knowledge prior to the reading.

2. **Narrative Writing.** Ask students to read one of the graphic novels, paying careful attention to the details and imagery used. Then ask each student to write his or her own summary of the story being told in this novel. Graphic novels without much dialogue provide an opportunity for students to create their own dialogue, based on what they know of the content and character. Not only does this engage students in thinking about the content, it also provides you with some assessment information. Based on the dialogue that the students write, you'll understand what they already know, what they misunderstand from the story, and what they do not yet know.

3. **Summarizing Information.** A third possible use of graphic novels involves writing summaries. Like oral retellings of readings, written summaries require that students consider the main ideas in a piece of text and use their own words to recap what they know (Frey, Fisher, & Hernandez, 2003). Students can discuss the graphic novel and the text they have read with a small group, and then create their own summaries. Alternatively, students could summarize the text and then create a compare-and-contrast graphic organizer in which they note the differences between their summary of the text and the way that the author/illustrator of the graphic novel summarized the text (e.g., Fisher & Frey, 2004).

4 Reviewing content. In addition to serving as fodder for written summaries, graphic novels can be used for review of content. While there are many reasons to review content—such as preparing for a test—graphic novels are especially useful for providing students with a review of past chapters. You can use a graphic novel from a previous chapter to review the major events in time or place, so that students can situate the new information they are reading in a context.

5 Analysis. Graphic novels often have a thematic strand that illustrates a specific point about the content being studied. This may take the form of irony, humor, or a more direct and formal approach to a historical event. In their analysis, students read the graphic novel with the intention of trying to understand the main point the author is trying to convey. This approach is particularly useful after students have covered the content in the main textbook. Encouraging students to pose questions about the text will help to uncover the main points.

For example:

- Why did the author choose this topic?
- What does this graphic novel tell me about the people we have studied? Does the story relate ideas about their society, culture, religion, government, military, or economy, or to other aspects of their life?
- Is the tone of the story humorous or serious?
- Do I like the people being presented?
- Does the author portray the characters in a positive or negative way?
- What conclusions do these ideas suggest?

Have students write a few sentences answering these questions. Then have them summarize what they believe is the main point of the graphic novel.

6 Visualizing. Have students skim the chapter or a particular section of the chapter. Students should then pick one person, one event, or one concept from the reading and create a graphic representation of it. Students could use a comic book style to illustrate their topic. Their work could be funny, sad, serious, satirical or any other tone that they wish. They can use text and dialogue or let the pictures alone tell the story. Another option would be to use other media for their depiction of the topic. Students could take pictures, make a computer slide-show presentation, make a video, or create a song to represent their topic.

These are just some of the many uses of graphic novels. As you introduce them into your class, you may discover more ways to use this popular art form to engage your students in a new method of learning while exercising the multiple literacies your students already possess. We welcome you to the world of learning through graphic novels!

Fisher, D., & Frey, N. (2004). *Improving adolescent literacy: Strategies at work.* Upper Saddle River, NJ: Merrill Education.

Frey, N., Fisher, D., & Hernandez, T. (2003). "What's the gist?" Summary writing for struggling adolescent writers. *Voices from the Middle, 11*(2), 43–49.

Graphic Novels for The American Journey: Early Years

The following pages contain additional information about each individual graphic novel. You will find background information, brief summaries of each novel, and two activities to help you guide your students' understanding of each graphic novel. The first activity is designed to help the student utilize the story presented to complete the assigned task. The second activity is more broadly focused, allowing students to make connections between the graphic novel and the larger historical context of the period.

Unit 1: The Americas: Worlds Meet

Tenochtitlán

Summary

Much of what we know about the early life of the Aztec and the founding of the great city of Tenochtitlán is based on myth. According to their earliest legends, the Aztec believed they were born in the center of the Earth and came into the world through seven caves. Their first settlement was Aztlán, which most likely existed along Mexico's northwest coast. Around A.D. 1116, the Aztec moved south. They wandered for more than 100 years, settling in neighboring cities until their aggressive ways convinced their hosts to force the Aztec to move on. Sometime around 1300, the Aztec reached the shores of Lake Texcoco in the Valley of Mexico. Because the best lands in the region were taken by more powerful peoples, the Aztec settled in swampy areas. Eventually, they began to build their great city on the island where, according to legend, they saw an eagle perched on a cactus.

Tenochtitlán quickly developed into a massive city, with huge temples and marketplaces. Wealthy priests, warriors, and traders led a highly organized society. By the time Hernán Cortés and his Spanish army arrived, Tenochtitlán had over 300,000 residents and stood at the center of an empire of some 6 million people. Following the Spanish invasion in 1519, however, the Aztec empire rapidly crumbled. Within two years, Aztec dominance in the region was destroyed. Although today, the splendor of Tenochtitlán lies buried beneath the streets of Mexico City, the legacy of the Aztec continues in many aspects of Mexican culture.

ACTIVITIES

1. Have students research the influence of the Aztec on modern Mexico's food, language, art, and culture. Ask students to list their findings and write a sentence or two about each.

2. Have students conduct further research into the Spanish conquest of Mexico. Ask students to write a short report explaining how a relatively small number of Spanish soldiers were able to defeat and destroy the Aztec Empire which consisted of about 6 million people. Ask: What was the Spaniards' reason for going to war against these people? What role do you think other people in the region played in the conquest?

THE SEA OF POSSIBILITIES

SUMMARY

This graphic novel opens with two sailors loading supplies onto their ship. They are discussing the possibilities of their voyage and disagreeing about what they are getting themselves into. One sailor is looking forward to the riches of Asia, while the other is considering the possibilities that there is something greater awaiting them in the ocean. Only toward the end do we discover that these sailors are sailing with Christopher Columbus on the Santa María.

ACTIVITIES

1. Ask students if they think the sailors on the *Santa María* will be successful finding a route to Asia. What do students think the sailors will find? Do they think the sailors will return home disappointed, or as heroes? Have students illustrate 3–4 panels using the characters from "The Sea of Possibilities" that depict what they think will happen to the sailors. The corresponding dialog for the panels should reflect the emotions and concerns of the sailors.

2. After reading the graphic novel, ask students to identify panels that explain what the captain and crew of the Santa María hoped to find on their voyage. Have students explain why discovering a western route to Asia was so important.

The Gentlemen of Jamestown

Summary

The English colonists who founded Jamestown colony remained anchored in the English Channel for weeks because of unfavorable winds. Even at that early point in the voyage, some of the aristocratic colonists wanted to turn back. Edward-Maria Wingfield, a noble, favored returning to England, but Captain John Smith, a commoner, argued against it. Wingfield thought Smith did not respect the opinions of his "betters" as he should. Smith, on the other hand, judged people according to their skills and their ability to deal with difficult situations. During the voyage, Wingfield accused Smith of mutiny. Existing records do not reveal the reason for this charge. It is likely Smith gave his unwanted opinions about something. Wingfield convinced Christopher Newport, captain of the *Susan Constant*, to arrest Smith. When hostilities again broke out between Smith and Wingfield over another unknown issue, Smith was nearly hung.

This graphic novel begins on the *Susan Constant* shortly before the colonists go ashore at the site chosen for the colony. After landing, Smith tries to have the colonists set up a safe and self-supporting colony. The gentlemen and Newport focus on following the Virginia Company's orders. Unfortunately, about half of the colonists do not understand they need to work hard if the colony is to survive. At the end of the novel, Smith is determined to make the colony a success.

Activities

1. The *Godspeed* was the second largest of the ships used by the Jamestown colonists. Fifty-two passengers and sailors lived on this ship for four months. The usable length of the deck was about 52 feet. The deck measured about 15 feet at its widest point. Ask students to make a space in the classroom that is proportional to the number of students in the class. For example, if there are 24–26 students, they would measure a space about 26 feet long and 7½ feet at its widest point. Remind them that a ship is curved in shape. Tell students to mark the space with masking tape. Have the class stand and/or sit inside the ship. As a class, discuss what it might have been like to live in this space for four months.

2. Ask students to read about the Jamestown colony in their textbooks. Discuss the reading in class. When did the colonists expect new supplies? When did the supplies actually arrive? What recurring events did the Jamestown colonists experience? Why did so many colonists die? Next, organize students into pairs. Have each pair make a graph. It should show the number of colonists who originally settled the colony and the rise and fall in population for the years 1607–1610. Pairs should also include calculations that demonstrate how they obtained their figures for the graphs.

Unit 2: Creating a Nation

Liberty's Stand

Summary

Each American colony had its own group of part-time militia. These men were not professional soldiers, but they participated in frequent training sessions, provided their own equipment, and were ready to gather and fight when needed. Some groups of militia called themselves "minutemen" because they claimed they could be ready on a minute's notice. In this graphic novel, a member of the militia has received notice that he is needed, and he is preparing his equipment. In the pages that follow, he explains to his daughter why he must leave her and be prepared to fight.

Activities

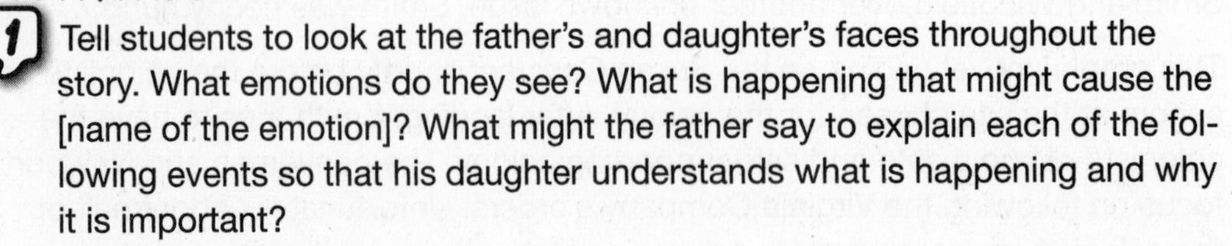

1. Tell students to look at the father's and daughter's faces throughout the story. What emotions do they see? What is happening that might cause the [name of the emotion]? What might the father say to explain each of the following events so that his daughter understands what is happening and why it is important?

    - the Boston Massacre
    - the Boston Tea Party
    - the battles at Lexington and Concord

    Next, organize the students into pairs. Tell the pairs to write narrative boxes and dialogue for this graphic novel. Their story should be historically accurate, but it should also demonstrate how the father and daughter feel about each other and the events. Have volunteers share their stories with the class.

2. After the class has read about the Boston Massacre, the Boston Tea Party, and the battles at Lexington and Concord, refer students to the graphic novel "Liberty's Stand." Help them determine that the father is explaining something to his daughter. Then as a class, choose which panels refer to the Boston Massacre, the Boston Tea Party, and the battles at Lexington and Concord. Have volunteers state facts that describe these events.

America's Citizen Soldiers

Summary

In August 1776, General George Washington and his Continental Army found themselves on the brink of defeat. Washington and his men had marched to Brooklyn, New York, to secure the mouth of the Hudson River, to prevent the British from gaining control of the waterway. British control would have cut New England off from the other colonies. Washington did not have a navy and his troops were poorly trained and ill-equipped.

King George sent the British fleet and the main British army, under the command of General William Howe. As weeks passed, thousands of British and German Hessian mercenary troops gathered in New York harbor. Howe's plan was to encircle the island with his ships, prevent Washington from escaping, and use his superior fire power to destroy the American forces. The British believed that would end the American Revolution. On August 29, Washington decided to retreat from Brooklyn. He realized he was hopelessly outnumbered and that he and his men would be massacred if they did not get off the island.

Washington asked General John Glover to organize and execute the evacuation of all 9,000 of the Continental Army's troops and their equipment. The men of Glover's regiment were all fishers by trade. That night a raging Nor'easter settled in. Along with the men of the Massachusetts 27th regiment, led by Israel Hutchinson, they spent the night in pouring rain and strong winds, rowing troops and their equipment, cannon, and horses across the East River to safety on the other side. Some military historians regard it as one of the most brilliant military retreats of all time.

Activities

1. Ask students to think about what might have happened if Glover and his troops had not been able to rescue Washington and his men. Then ask them to illustrate and narrate two or three panels depicting their opinions.

2. Ask students about the roles citizen soldiers fill in the United States today, especially following natural emergencies like floods, hurricanes, tornadoes, and forest fires. Discuss the sacrifices that these citizens make when they are called to duty, what kind of jobs they hold in their everyday lives, and how their families are impacted when they do get the call to serve. Ask students to write a paragraph about why they think a person would want to be a citizen soldier.

We the People

Summary

This graphic novel illustrates the drafting of the United States Constitution. The purpose of this graphic novel is to familiarize students with some of the important participants, positions, and compromises involved in writing the Constitution. While the Constitution was drafted and signed by the delegates in 1787, it was not ratified until 1790. Three delegates—Elbridge Gerry of Massachusetts, and Edmund Randolph and George Mason of Virginia—did not sign the Constitution in 1787. Gerry and Mason specifically did not sign because they wanted to add a bill of rights. Some states were hesitant to ratify the Constitution until they were assured that a bill of rights would be added as amendments. The Bill of Rights would be added to the Constitution in 1791.

Activities

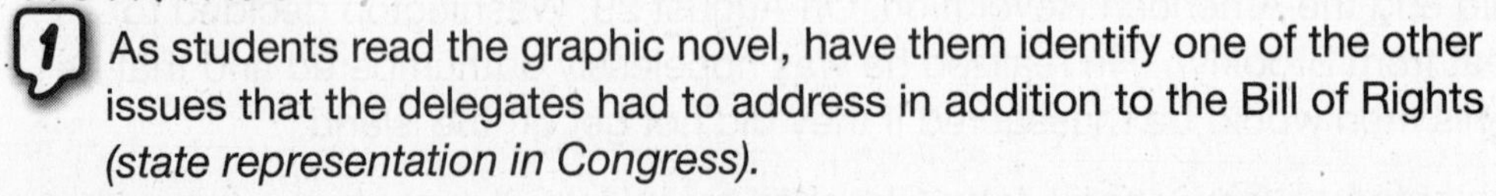

1. As students read the graphic novel, have them identify one of the other issues that the delegates had to address in addition to the Bill of Rights *(state representation in Congress).*

2. Organize students into groups. Ask each group to research the events of the Constitutional Convention. Have each group write and act in a play about the Constitutional Convention. The play might include people debating why a bill of rights should be added to the Constitution and include the characters of Gerry, Randolph, and Mason. Other themes might address the rights of women and slavery. After each group has presented its play, ask the class to evaluate whether the group effectively presented the different opinions about the play's theme.

Unit 3: Launching the Republic

Washington's America

Summary

George Washington led the American army during the Revolutionary War. He helped the thirteen colonies win their independence from the strongest power in the world. In 1789 Washington was elected as the first president of the United States. He led the American army and the country at times when it was uncertain whether the United States would continue to exist as a nation. During both those times, Washington had to solve many problems that the country had never dealt with before. This graphic novel shows Washington toward the end of his presidency. He is sharing his personal experiences and his opinions about the United States and its future.

Activities

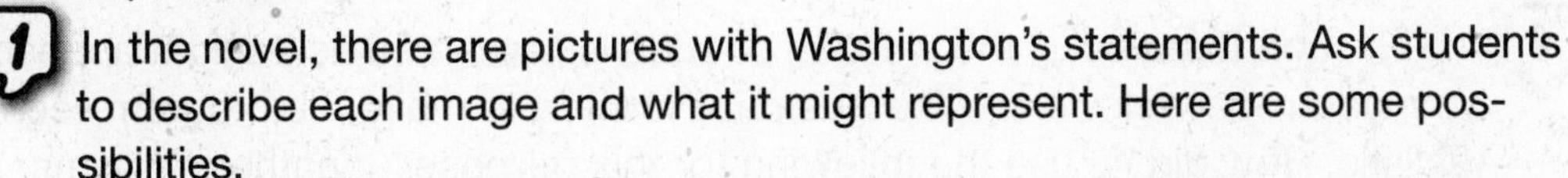

1. In the novel, there are pictures with Washington's statements. Ask students to describe each image and what it might represent. Here are some possibilities.

    - Flying eagle: It is the country's national bird. It might stand for freedom.
    - Declaration of Independence: The Patriots declared their independence from Britain. Now no king can take their rights away.

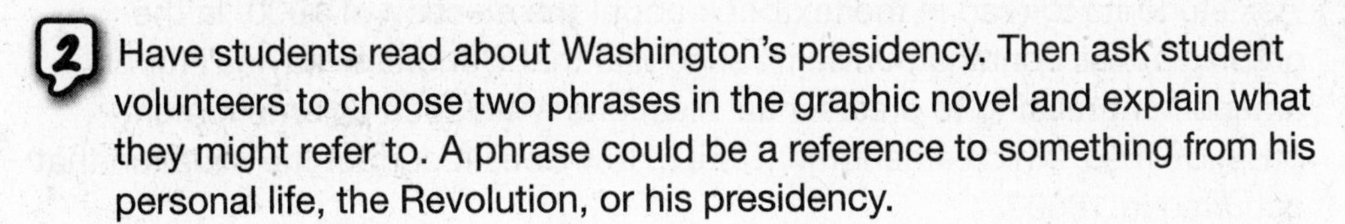

2. Have students read about Washington's presidency. Then ask student volunteers to choose two phrases in the graphic novel and explain what they might refer to. A phrase could be a reference to something from his personal life, the Revolution, or his presidency.

Election Deadlock!: An ANN Special Report

Summary

In the presidential election of 1800, the Electoral College provided a challenge for the young republic. But what is the Electoral College? Why was it created? During the Constitutional Convention, there were debates about how to choose the most qualified people for president and vice president. It was considered dangerous to let people vote directly for these offices. Instead, the framers had states choose electors. A state would have electors equal to the total number of its representatives and senators. Each state could decide how to choose its electors. In the early days of the country, the state legislature usually selected its electors.

The electors from all the states were known as the Electoral College. After a presidential election, the Electoral College would meet to vote for the president and vice president. Each elector could vote for two candidates. Only one of them could come from his own state. To become president, a candidate had to receive a majority of the electors' votes and the greatest number of votes. The runner-up became vice president. The electors had no way to show that they wanted one candidate for president and another for vice president. This weakness in the system resulted in Thomas Jefferson and Aaron Burr receiving the same number of electoral votes in the election of 1800.

The graphic novel "Election Deadlock" begins towards the end of Election Day, 1800. The anchorperson, Jonathan Williams, describes the election returns. Jefferson and Burr are tied for president. Then his expert guest, Samuel Williamson, explains why a tie could happen. After a six-day wait, Williams updates citizens on the situation. Then Williamson comments on what may be going on behind the scenes. Finally, the deadlock is broken, and Jefferson is elected president.

Activities

1. In "Election Deadlock," the election of 1800 is presented as it might appear on modern-day television. The illustrator wanted to make the program seem realistic. How did he use the following for this purpose: Jonathan Williams, Samuel Williamson, dialogue, pictures, and labels? Was the illustrator successful? Why or why not? Ask students to add a couple frames showing either candidate's reaction to the results.

2. Ask students to read in the textbook about the election of 1800. In the graphic novel, Jonathan Williams suggests that Congress may call for an amendment relating to presidential elections. Was such an amendment passed? If so, which amendment is it? How does it correct the situation that occurred in 1800?

On Her Own

Summary

The girls who worked in the factories in Lowell were not just from Massachusetts. They came from what were then considered distant places, such as Maine, New Hampshire, and Vermont. These workers had a variety of reasons for working in the mills. Some girls were saving their wages to help pay for the things they would need after they were married. Other girls were helping put male family members through college. Still other girls had more social reasons for working. Some wanted access to lending libraries and interesting lectures. Others sought extra money for buying fashionable clothes. On average, most girls worked in the mills for about three years. In this graphic novel, a teenage girl named Abby moves to Lowell and learns what working in a factory is like. She also makes new friends and experiences city life. By the end of "On Her Own," Abby understands both the positives and negatives of being a "Lowell girl."

Activities

1. Discuss with the class the opening scene between Abby and her father. Ask students questions such as: How does Abby's father feel about her working in Lowell? Why do you believe that? How does Abby try to relieve her father's concerns? Then point out that at the end of the novel, Abby is trying to decide whether to stay in Lowell or go home. Next, organize the class into pairs and have each pair go through the story, making a list of reasons to support each of Abby's choices. Finally, pairs should use the information in their lists to draw several panels in which they show what Abby decides to do and why.

2 Tell students to read about economic growth during the Industrial Revolution and its effects on New England and the lives of the Lowell girls. Ask students to suggest reasons why Abby's family needed the wages she could earn in a factory. Point out that Abby's parents also probably grew up on small farms. When Abby's parents were teenagers, could they have helped their parents by working in a factory? Why or why not? Why did Abby probably choose Lowell as the best place to look for a factory job? Was the factory where Abby and her friends worked a typical factory? Why or why not?

Unit 4: Nationalism and Sectionalism

Sequoya and the Cherokee Nation

Summary

The Cherokee lived mostly in North Carolina, Tennessee, and Georgia. Many white Americans settled near them, and the Cherokee wanted to show that they were not dangerous. During the late 1700s and early 1800s, they, therefore, adopted many of the ways of white Americans.

A Cherokee named Sequoya wanted to create a written form of the Cherokee language. He borrowed some letters from English. He changed some of those letters, and he invented new ones. Sequoya assigned a different letter to each separate sound in the Cherokee language. When he was done, there were 86 symbols and a system for reading and writing Cherokee. Many Cherokee learned to read and write their language. In 1828 Sequoya and a minister named Samuel Worcester began printing a newspaper called the *Cherokee Phoenix.*

The Cherokee also developed a government similar to that of the United States. Their government had judicial, legislative, and executive branches. The graphic novel "Sequoya and the Cherokee Nation" shows Cherokee attempts to adapt to white American ways. In addition, the novel includes their legal fight against forced relocation and ends with the Trail of Tears.

Activities

Ask students to read all except the last two pages of "Sequoya and the Cherokee Nation." Ask students why the Cherokee adopted white American ways. What kinds of changes did they make? How did they feel about these changes? Have students look at the last two pages of the novel. Ask students how the Cherokee used the U.S. legal system to stay on their lands. Is the illustrator sympathetic toward Jackson or the Cherokee? Have students defend their opinions with examples—pictures and text—from the novel.

2 Ask students to read about the removal of the Cherokee and the other four "Civilized Tribes" from the Southeastern United States. Why did white Americans want Cherokee lands? Was Jackson for or against relocation? Tell students to look at the last three frames in the graphic novel. How did Jackson react to the Supreme Court's decision? How do you know if Jackson carried out the Court's decision? What does the relocation of the Cherokee show about the relationship between the Supreme Court and the president at this time?

From Sea to Shining Sea

Summary

The concept of Manifest Destiny became popular in the United States during the 1840s. There were idealistic and practical reasons behind the belief that the United States should posses all of North America. White Americans believed that democracy was the best kind of government. They thought that it was their duty to spread democratic ideas. On the practical side, the white population of the United States had grown greatly from around 5 million in 1800 to more than 23 million in the mid-1800s. Since most of these people were farmers, the country needed land for them. The vast, open areas that belonged to British Canada and Mexico seemed to be natural places into which the United States could expand. In this graphic novel, a father and son attend a speech given by the president. It focuses on the spread of the United States from the Atlantic Ocean to the Pacific. The president's speech honors mostly white Americans whose efforts have made this achievement possible. The father is impressed by the speech. The son, however, wonders about the personal costs to the people who were affected by these events.

Activities

In his speech, the president names several places that Americans fought for or acquired in some other way. Ask students why they think the president has a map hanging behind him. Whose contributions does the president especially want remembered? Then have students explain the following:

- Why the president compared the expansion of the United States to pieces in a puzzle.
- Whether "From Sea to Shining Sea" is an appropriate title for this graphic novel.

Finally, ask volunteers to research—either in a book of quotations, such as *Bartlett's Familiar Quotations*, or online—the origin of the expression "from sea to shining sea."

2 Remind the class that the United States bought the Louisiana Territory from France. Tell students to list the other places and purchases shown on the map behind the president. Have the students use their textbooks and other sources to determine the following about each area:

- Any other country or countries that claimed the area.
- How the United States gained control of the area.

As a class, have students use this information and their own background knowledge to answer the questions that the son asks on the last page of the graphic novel.

Strangers on a Train

Summary

Starting in colonial times, the North and the South developed different economies. Climate, geography, and resources contributed to these differences. In this graphic novel, a Portuguese businessman, Vitor Romão, is traveling to Raleigh, North Carolina. He is looking for investment opportunities in the United States. On the train, he meets the Miller family from the North and a man from the South. Both Mr. Miller and the Southerner have very good reasons why Mr. Romão should invest in their region of the country. The conversation ends when the Millers and the Southerner change to a different train.

Activities

Remind students that a story needs a plot, one or more characters, and a setting. Explain that in the beginning an author may only have a general idea of what she wants to write about. The idea might be as simple as what it was like to be a colonist at Jamestown or what Valley Forge was like in the winter of 1777–1778. Ask students what the general topic of "Strangers on a Train" is. Next, point out that for this story, the writer had to figure out a realistic way to bring Northerners and Southerners (the characters) together. He needed to provide a reason why they would talk about their economies. Then ask questions such as the following: Whose ideas do the Millers present? Why do you think the author chose a train as the *setting*, or location, for the story? Is it important that Romão is a foreigner? Why or why not? How does this help the *plot*, the action in the story, move along? Is the train an effective setting for this story? Why or why not? Then organize students into small groups. Tell each group to create several frames for "Strangers on a Train." They should show where Mr. Romão decided to invest and why he made that decision.

2 After students have read Chapter 13 of the textbook and "Strangers on a Train," hold a brief class discussion on the differences between the North and the South at the time of the story, especially economic differences. Then have students form small groups. Each group will act as a "public relations firm" for either the North or the South. Using their textbooks and outside resources, student groups should create short presentations emphasizing the benefits of living in/investing in one of the regions in the pre-Civil War era. Students should expand on the issues raised in the novel, offering more details, facts, and figures in their presentations. Have groups present their information to the class. Then discuss which region, North or South, appeared to offer better opportunities at the time.

Unit 5: Civil War and Reconstruction

Seeing the Light

Summary

In the years leading up to the Civil War, our nation was battling with the issue of slavery. Violence broke out in many cities between those who supported slavery and the abolitionists who opposed it. Several court rulings and laws added to the tension, as the government tried to determine the best way to keep peace among the states. As the nation grew, adding states and new territories became increasingly difficult as both sides were vying for power.

While the government was debating what to do, average Americans were finding ways to help the antislavery movement. Many risked their lives and broke laws to assist enslaved African Americans escaping from Southern bondage. The Underground Railroad, a series of secret paths dotted with safe houses and helpful people, played a key role in helping many people escape enslavement and get out of the South.

This graphic novel tells the story of a husband and wife, who are just average Americans struggling with the decision to help escaped African Americans on the Underground Railroad. The story shows the couple trying to take on this commitment, while also showing the escape efforts of an enslaved worker heading north. The Northern wife wishes to help, while the husband is more reluctant. However, when he is confronted by the brutal reality of one enslaved woman's experience, he becomes committed to the effort. The end of the graphic novel shows several ways that people secretly escaped the South—hiding in secret wagon compartments or in cellars and barns, or looking for the symbols and signs (like a lantern in the window) that signaled that a house was a safe haven.

Activities

1. When the husband in the novel realizes that the escaped slave is a girl, he is shocked. When he sees that she was badly hurt he is immediately ready to assist. Having never personally faced the reality of slavery, he had not realized how horribly enslaved people were treated nor had he realized that they were not just men, but women and children too. Have the students change the enslaved character to a man, and speculate if the story would continue in the same direction or change in any way.

2. One issue causing the division of the Union was slavery. The two sides could not compromise, and separation was looming. This chapter in the textbook discusses the debate on secession in greater detail. Discuss what issues could arise in creating separate countries on common soil with a common history.

Fort Sumter's Last Stand

Summary

Some Southerners viewed the election of Abraham Lincoln in November 1860 as a threat to the Southern way of life. South Carolina, the location of Fort Sumter, was the first state to secede from the Union in December 1860.

In an effort to compromise, Senator John J. Crittenden of Kentucky proposed amendments to the Constitution in December 1860. The amendments would guarantee slavery where it already existed and reinstate the Missouri Compromise line, while extending it all the way to the California border. Slavery would be permitted south of the line, while it was prohibited north of the line. Crittenden's compromise effort was not successful.

By February 1, 1861, six states from the Lower South had seceded. A week later the seceding states declared themselves a new nation—the Confederate States of America. Jefferson Davis was selected to be president, and Confederate forces began seizing federal lands within the South. Fort Sumter, located in Charleston Harbor in South Carolina, remained occupied by federal troops.

Lincoln stated in his inaugural address that he intended to "hold, occupy, and possess" federal property in seceded states. In April Lincoln announced he was going to resupply Fort Sumter. Davis decided the Confederacy should take Fort Sumter before the supply ship arrived. Confederate leaders delivered a note to Major Robert Anderson demanding Fort Sumter's surrender by the morning of April 12, 1861. Major Anderson stood his ground and the Confederate forces bombarded Fort Sumter for 33 hours before Major Anderson finally surrendered.

This story is told from the perspective of the wife of a U.S. Army officer stationed at Fort Sumter. She is reading a letter written by her husband describing the events at the fort in the weeks leading up to the bombardment.

Activities

1. Letter writing was the primary form of communication between separated families. Have students write letters to their families as if they were members of the Confederate forces preparing to attack Fort Sumter. Make sure students explain why the Confederates wanted to attack Fort Sumter.

2. As states in the Lower South seceded, Congress tried to find a compromise to save the Union. Have students explain Crittenden's Compromise and why it did not succeed.

The Impeachment of Andrew Johnson

Summary

The United States Constitution gives Congress the power to remove any federal official from office who has committed a serious offense. The process requires a majority vote of the members of the House of Representatives to impeach, or accuse, an official of misconduct. The official is then brought to trial in front of the Senate, where his guilt or innocence will be decided. All Senate members serve on the jury. After hearing the evidence, the members vote on whether or not the official is guilty. Conviction requires a two-thirds majority vote.

Using a television interview format, this graphic novel examines the impeachment trial of President Andrew Johnson. As the story begins, President Johnson has already been impeached by the House of Representatives, meaning he has been accused of official misconduct. The Senate has conducted the trial and is getting ready to vote on the president's guilt or innocence.

Outside the Senate, shortly before the vote takes place, a young reporter is interviewing both Johnson's supporters and his accusers, who are led by the fiery congressional representative, Thaddeus Stevens. Their arguments should sound somewhat familiar. Stevens argues that Johnson has abused the powers of his office and should be removed. Johnson's supporters, however, feel that he inherited some very difficult issues, like Reconstruction in the South and civil rights for the newly freed slaves, and that he is doing the very best he can. They claim Johnson is just a victim of Washington politics.

Many people across the country are unhappy with the job the president is doing. But did he commit any crimes that would justify removing him from office? That is what the members of the Senate have to decide.

Activities

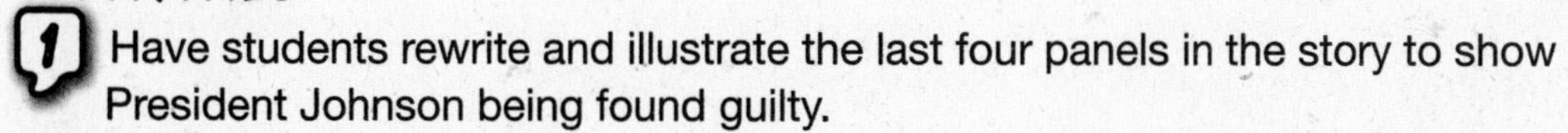

1. Have students rewrite and illustrate the last four panels in the story to show President Johnson being found guilty.

2. Have your students refer to their textbooks and make a list of the powers that have been granted to Congress. Then have them choose one particular power on their list and write a paragraph about it explaining how that power affects them and their family.

UNIT 1

The Americas: Worlds Meet

MEXICO CITY, 2006.
TODAY, MEXICO CITY, WITH OVER 8 MILLION PEOPLE, IS ONE OF THE LARGEST CITIES IN THE WORLD. HUNDREDS OF YEARS AGO, HOWEVER, THE AREA WAS A MARSHY LAKE.

ACCORDING TO LEGEND, AN EAGLE WITH A SNAKE IN ITS BEAK LED AN ANCIENT PEOPLE TO BUILD A GREAT CITY ON THAT MARSHY LAND.

IT IS BELIEVED THAT THE AZTEC ARRIVED IN THE CENTRAL VALLEY OF MEXICO AROUND A.D. 1200.
WARRIORS?
WE DON'T WANT THEIR KIND HERE.

STAY CLOSE, CHILDREN.
WHEN THE AZTEC FIRST ARRIVED, THE PEOPLE WHO ALREADY LIVED THERE DID NOT WANT THEM TO SETTLE IN THE AREA. THEY WERE AFRAID OF THE AZTEC.

WHAT ARE WE GONNA DO? NOBODY LIKES US!
RELAX, WE'RE THE AZTEC. WE ARE ACCUSTOMED TO A NOMADIC WAY OF LIFE.
ONE DAY OUR GOD HUITZILOPOCHTLI WILL LEAD US TO THE PROMISED LAND.

HUITZILOPOCHTLI

WE HAVE HELPED YOU TO DEFEAT YOUR ENEMIES, CHIEF, JUST AS YOU REQUESTED.

THE CHIEFS OF SOME OF THE NEARBY CITY-STATES OFTEN ASKED THE AZTEC TO HELP SUBDUE THEIR WARRING NEIGHBORS. WHEN THE AZTEC DID AS THEY WERE ASKED, THEY WERE REWARDED AND ALLOWED TO STAY A LITTLE LONGER.

I WILL GIVE YOU THIS FINE PIECE OF LAND.
HEH HEH HEH.

EVENTUALLY ONE KING REWARDED THEM WITH A BARREN PIECE OF LAND INFESTED WITH POISONOUS SNAKES.

HE THOUGHT THAT THE SNAKES WOULD DESTROY THE AZTEC.

THE AZTEC ROASTED THE SNAKES AND PROSPERED.

THE AZTEC SETTLED FOR A WHILE, BUT WHEN THEY CAME UNDER ATTACK FROM A MUCH LARGER ARMY, THEY FLED TO THE MARSHES AROUND LAKE TEXCOCO.
UH OH.

LEGEND SAYS THAT THEY SAW THE PROMISED SIGN FROM THEIR GOD HUITZILOPOCHTLI. THIS IS WHERE THEY WOULD MAKE THEIR HOME.
LOOK! ON THAT CACTUS! THE EAGLE EATING A SNAKE! WE'RE HERE!

WE HAVE BUILT A MAGNIFICENT CITY. THE BIGGEST TEMPLE WAS BUILT TO HONOR YOU, HUITZILOPOCHTLI.
EXCELLENT!
YOU WILL CALL THIS CITY TENOCHTITLÁN.
TENOCHTITLÁN? WHAT DOES IT MEAN?
IT MEANS "PLACE OF THE PRICKLY PEAR CACTUS."

IT WAS PERFECT. ALTHOUGH IT WAS CLOSE TO THE EQUATOR, THE ALTITUDE KEPT THE TEMPERATURE ABOUT 65 DEGREES YEAR ROUND.

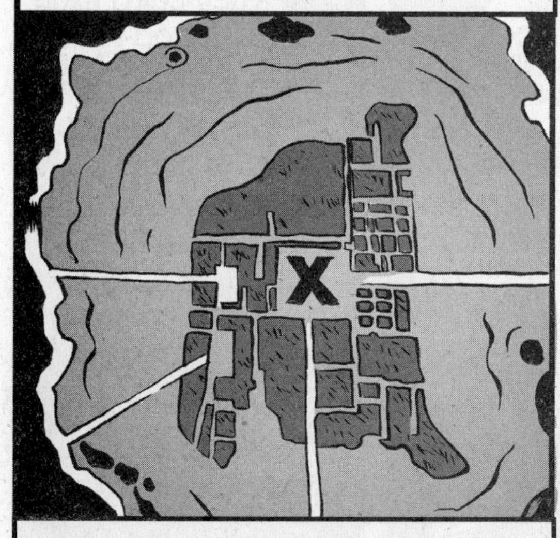

THE SURROUNDING WATER OF THE LAKE PROTECTED THE CITY FROM ATTACK. AN AQUEDUCT BROUGHT FRESH WATER FROM THE MOUNTAINS.

THE LAKE'S WATERS ALSO PROVIDED FOOD, INCLUDING EDIBLE ALGAE...

...UNTIL ABOUT 1519.
FANTASTIC!
HERNÁN CORTÉS
BERNAL DÍAZ DEL CASTILLO

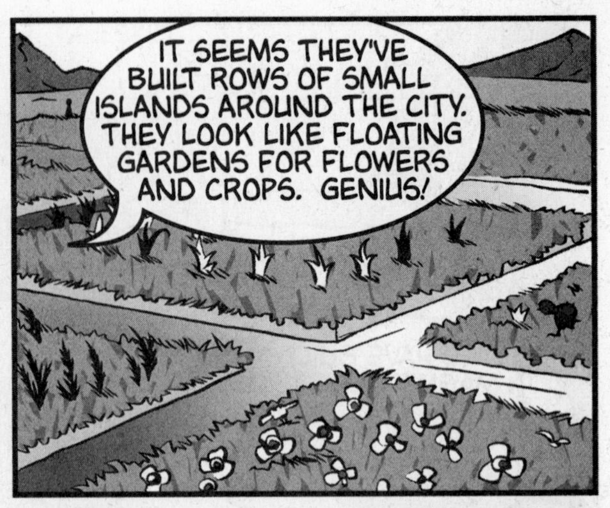
IT SEEMS THEY'VE BUILT ROWS OF SMALL ISLANDS AROUND THE CITY. THEY LOOK LIKE FLOATING GARDENS FOR FLOWERS AND CROPS. GENIUS!

I LOVE THE SMELL OF TENOCHTITLÁN IN THE MORNING.
WOW! LOOK, ROOFTOP FLOWER GARDENS...

...FILLED WITH BEAUTIFUL FLOWERS AND PLANTS.

AND THEY HAVE AVIARIES FILLED WITH THOUSANDS OF SPECIES OF BIRDS.

THEY EVEN HAVE A ZOO FILLED WITH CARNIVORES AND REPTILES.

Dear King,

Today we sa
city of gold
huge temple
many sma
Twenty thou
cleanest st

UNIT 1

The Americas: Worlds Meet

I can see it now - "Antonio Lopez - Sailor of the Year"! Woo hoo!

Fame and fortune, here we come! We'll be heroes!
Heroes? I don't know about that.

Ha! This may be your first time on the high seas, but don't let that stop ya from thinkin' BIG!
If we find that western route to Asia, the way the Captain said..
WHOA!

People will be lining up to buy what we bring back - silks, spices, you name it!
I know.... I know all that. It's just....

Just WHAT? We'll be able to sell everything CHEAPER, too, because the trip takes less time. Going overland - feh, it's for the birds!

I see what you're saying, Antonio...
It's just...do we REALLY know what we're getting ourselves into?

Ha! Goin' to sea's always a risk. Do ya really believe those old wives' tales about the earth being FLAT? Captain's got me convinced, just like he convinced the Queen.
THE UNKNOWN
EUROPE
ASIA

But think about it: has anyone ever tried this...
...and come home again?

Oh, come off it! Rest assured, the Cap'n knows EXACTLY what he's doin'....
I don't doubt that...

A real THINKER we got here...humph! Don't worry, kid, once you get your sea legs you'll forget all about this!

I'm sorry, I guess I'm just thinkin' out loud...just trying to weigh the risks against the possibilities...
...the BIGGER possibilities.

Bigger? And what could be BIGGER than a route to Asia and all its riches? The kingdom of heaven? Ha!

I don't know for sure, but anything's possible.
We're sailing out into the biggest body of water known to man!

Just look at it- it's HUGE!
And even when we've sailed out to its farthest reaches, what then? There could be a whole new world out there!

I'll solve your mystery right now, buddy - that new world, it's ASIA!
You kids!
POW

Come on, this is the last one. 'What else is out there?' Ha...you've got to calm down, amigo, and take a good deep breath.
After all, this is the last Spanish air we're going to be breathin' for a while.

Enjoy it while you can!

SANTA MARIA
I guess Antonio's right...
This is probably going to be a pretty boring voyage.
Probably....
ellen lindner 2005

UNIT 1

The Americas: Worlds Meet

APRIL 26, 1607. AFTER A LONG, DIFFICULT OCEAN VOYAGE, WE ARRIVED IN THE LAND OF VIRGINIA.
GUARDS, RELEASE THE PRISONER.

WELCOME BACK TO DAYLIGHT, SMITH. I HOPE YOU'VE LEARNED A LESSON ABOUT QUESTIONING YOUR BETTERS.
I WOULDN'T COUNT ON IT, WINGFIELD. WHY ARE YOU LETTING ME OUT?
A COUPLE WEEKS AGO, YOU WERE TRYING TO PERSUADE ME TO STICK MY NECK IN A NOOSE.

SADLY, THAT IS NOT TO BE. CAPTAIN NEWPORT'S ORDERS. HE JUST BROKE THE SEAL ON OUR CHARTER FROM THE VIRGINIA COMPANY.
AND WHAT DOES IT SAY?

OH, ABOUT WHAT YOU'D EXPECT. FIND A COLONY SITE. BE FRIENDLY TO THE LOCALS. LOOK FOR GOLD AND FIND A PASSAGE TO THE INDIES.
NONE OF WHICH REQUIRES LETTING ME OUT.

YES, WELL, THE CHARTER ALSO LISTS THE BOARD OF GOVERNORS FOR THE COLONY. MOSTLY FINE GENTLEMEN, SUCH AS GOSNOLD AND MYSELF...
AND?
SUSAN CONSTANT
IT MUST'VE BEEN A MISTAKE. PERHAPS THE INVESTORS MEANT ANOTHER JOHN SMITH.

WHY WOULD THEY APPOINT A COMMONER TO A RULING COUNCIL?
HAH!
MAYBE THE INVESTORS HAVE SOME BRAINS AFTER ALL.
DON'T GET TOO EXCITED. YOU'RE OUT OF THE BRIG, BUT YOU'RE STILL UNDER ARREST UNTIL WE CAN FIND WORK SUITABLE FOR SOMEONE LIKE YOU.

MAY 14.
IS IT SETTLED THEN, CAPTAIN NEWPORT? IS THIS THE COLONY SITE?
YES! IT'S FLAT AND UNINHABITED, NEAR THE WATER, BUT FAR ENOUGH FROM THE SEA THAT THE SPANISH CAN'T ATTACK THE COLONY.
WE LEARNED LATER WHY THIS AREA WAS UNINHABITED. IT WAS MOSTLY MARSHLAND WITH NO SAFE DRINKING WATER. IT WAS HOT, HUMID, AND FILLED WITH GREAT BLACK CLOUDS OF DISEASE-CARRYING MOSQUITOES. LITTLE WONDER NO ONE LIVED THERE!
AH, YES.
THIS WILL DO ADMIRABLY.
SMITH, HERE'S A JOB YOU'RE FIT FOR: CONSTRUCTION. WE'LL NEED SOME HUTS OR SOMETHING.
YES, SIR. AND A HIGH FENCE. AND SOME GARDENS.
YOU MEN, GRAB SOME TOOLS. I NEED YOUR HELP WITH THE BUILDING.
DON'T BE ABSURD. WE'RE GENTRY! WORK IS BENEATH US.
IDLENESS IS OUR BIRTHRIGHT. DIDN'T WE BRING YOUR KIND OVER TO TAKE CARE OF THAT SORT OF THING?
I'M GLAD TO SEE YOU MEN WORKING. WE'LL NEED THOSE TREES TO BUILD THE HUTS.
SORRY, CAPTAIN SMITH. WE'RE CUTTING LUMBER TO SHIP BACK HOME.
COMPANY ORDERS. WE NEED TO MAKE A GOOD RETURN FOR OUR INVESTORS, RIGHT?

AND YOU?
WE'RE LOOKING FOR GOLD!
THIS IS MADNESS! THIS IS NO TIME TO BE WORRIED ABOUT PROFIT! OR TO PLAY GAMES! WE HAVE NO HOUSES, NO CROPS, AND WE'RE UTTERLY DEFENSELESS! WHAT IF THE LOCALS ATTACKED? WHAT CHANCE WOULD THIS COLONY HAVE?
PIFFLE! THE LOCALS WHO VISITED EARLIER LOOKED PERFECTLY FRIENDLY. WE DON'T WANT TO OFFEND THEM BY LOOKING LIKE WE DON'T TRUST THEM, NOW DO WE? THAT'S WHY, AS PRESIDENT OF THE COUNCIL, I ORDERED THAT ALL OF OUR GUNS SHOULD STAY PACKED UP IN THEIR BOXES.
IT'S A LITTLE THING CALLED DIPLOMACY, SMITH. I DON'T EXPECT YOU TO HAVE HEARD OF IT.
MAY 20TH. WE ENGAGED IN DIPLOMATIC RELATIONS WITH A LOCAL GROUP. THEIR MEN AND OURS DID NOT GET ALONG WITH ONE ANOTHER.
TO BE SURE, I DON'T THINK THEY GOT MY JOKES.

MAY 21ST. ONE OF OUR INSTRUCTIONS FROM THE INVESTORS WAS TO LOOK FOR A WATER PASSAGE TO THE INDIES.
CAPTAIN NEWPORT, THERE'S SO MUCH BUILDING TO DO. AND PLANTING. WE NEED ALL THE MEN HERE.
COMPANY ORDERS, SMITH. AND YOU'RE COMING, TOO.
AND SO WE SET OFF WITH 23 MEN TO EXPLORE THE JAMES RIVER.
WE SOON MET A HUNTING PARTY WHO DREW US A MAP OF THE AREA.
falls
LATER, OTHER LOCALS TOLD US THAT ALL THIS LAND IS CONTROLLED BY ONE GREAT CHIEF. HIS NAME IS POWHATAN.
MAY 27TH. WE REACHED THE WATER-FALL AND COULD GO NO FURTHER.
ALRIGHT. THAT'S FAR ENOUGH. LET'S SEE HOW THEY'RE DOING AT HOME.
MEANWHILE, BACK AT JAMESTOWN...
UNPACK THE GUNS! UNPACK THE GUNS!

AND SO I, PRESIDENT EDWARD-MARIA WINGFIELD, DECLARE THAT WE SHALL BUILD A *FORT.* WITH A NICE, FORTIFIED *WALL*...
AND *CANNONS!*
COULD SOMEONE LOOK INTO A MOAT?
MAY 28, 1607. THE FOLLOWING DAYS WERE FILLED WITH LONG HOURS OF FRANTIC CONSTRUCTION...
IT'S A HAMMER.
PUNCTUATED BY SUDDEN, UNPREDICTABLE ATTACKS BY SMALL PARTIES OF LOCALS.
WITH THE CONSTANT THREAT OF ATTACK, IT WAS IMPOSSIBLE TO REST, WHICH MADE THE WORK ALL THE MORE TIRING.
JUNE 4TH. FINALLY...
AHH. I'LL SLEEP EASIER TONIGHT.
YE GODS! I HAVE A BLISTER!
NOW, *YOU LOT,* GET BACK TO CUTTING LUMBER!

JUNE 22ND. WE HAD FINALLY MADE SOME PROGRESS TOWARDS ESTABLISHING A COLONY. THINGS WERE LOOKING UP.
CAPTAIN NEWPORT SAILED FOR ENGLAND TO DELIVER OUR LUMBER.
AND THEN ALL WORK STOPPED.
WHAT DO YOU EXPECT? ALL THE SAILORS WENT BACK WITH NEWPORT.
THAT'S RIGHT. THERE'S **NO ONE LEFT** TO DO THE WORK!
BUT WE NEED TO GROW SOME **FOOD** AND DIG SOME WELLS FOR **FRESH WATER!**
WHY BOTHER? THE SHIPS WILL BE BACK IN NOVEMBER WITH **OODLES** OF SUPPLIES.
WHOSE IDEA WAS IT TO SEND GENTLEMEN TO START A COLONY? WE'RE STARVING, AND DISEASE IS BEGINNING TO SPREAD. THEY WON'T BREAK A SWEAT, EVEN WHEN THEIR OWN LIVES ARE AT STAKE.
I SAY, WHO'S UP FOR A ROUSING GAME OF CARDS?
SOON I'LL HEAD OUT TO TRY AND FIND THIS CHIEF POWHATAN. WE'LL NEED TO ESTABLISH FRIENDLY RELATIONS AND TRADE FOR FOOD IF THIS COLONY IS GOING TO SURVIVE.
THE GENTLEMEN OF JAMESTOWN MAY SCORN ME AS THEIR INFERIOR, BUT I WILL SPEND ALL MY STRENGTH AND EFFORT TRYING TO KEEP THE COLONY ALIVE **DESPITE THEM.**

Unit 2

Creating a Nation

UNIT 2

Creating a Nation

AUGUST, 1776. BROOKLYN, NEW YORK
GEORGE WASHINGTON'S CONTINENTAL ARMY IS TRAPPED ON LONG ISLAND. THE BRITISH FLEET IS IN THE HARBOR, WAITING FOR THE WIND TO CHANGE DIRECTION SO THAT THEY CAN ENCIRCLE THE ISLAND AND PREVENT WASHINGTON'S ESCAPE. THOUSANDS OF BRITISH AND HESSIAN SOLDIERS ARE MARCHING TOWARDS WASHINGTON'S TROOPS.
GENERAL WASHINGTON KNOWS HE IS OUTNUMBERED AND MUST RETREAT, OR HIS ARMY WILL BE DESTROYED. THERE IS ONLY ONE THING TO DO...
THE BRITISH ARE CLOSE, SIR. WE DON'T HAVE MUCH TIME, AND BAD WEATHER IS MOVING IN.

IF GENERAL HOWE AND HIS REDCOATS DEFEAT US HERE, THE REVOLUTION IS OVER. THEY WILL KILL OR CAPTURE US ALL.
FIND GENERAL GLOVER AND ASK HIM TO REPORT AT ONCE.
HOW CAN GENERAL GLOVER HELP?
THE MEN IN JOHN GLOVER'S MARBLEHEADERS REGIMENT ARE ALL SEAMEN BY TRADE. THEY ARE TOUGH AND WELL-DISCIPLINED. WE NEED THEM TO FERRY US ACROSS THE EAST RIVER TONIGHT, UNDER THE COVER OF DARKNESS AND THE APPROACHING STORM.
ALL OF US! BUT, SIR, WE HAVE OVER 9000 MEN TO TRANSPORT, PLUS THEIR EQUIPMENT, THE CANNON, AND THE HORSES. IS IT POSSIBLE?
IT HAS TO BE.

WITH FIGHTING IN THE DISTANCE, THE MESSENGER SETS OFF TO FIND GENERAL GLOVER AND HIS REGIMENT.

I MUST HURRY, DANGER IS EVERYWHERE. AH, THERE THEY ARE!

GENERAL GLOVER, THANK YOU FOR COMING. YOUR COUNTRY REALLY NEEDS YOU THIS NIGHT.
WHAT CAN I DO?
WE MUST ESCAPE FROM THIS ISLAND. WE ARE HOPELESSLY OUTNUMBERED AND FACE CERTAIN DEATH IF WE STAY AND CONTINUE TO FIGHT. CAN YOU GET US ACROSS THE RIVER?
YES, BUT WE MUST HURRY. A NOR'EASTER IS MOVING IN. IT WILL BRING HEAVY RAIN AND A LOT OF WIND, BUT IT WILL ALSO SLOW THE BRITISH AND GIVE US SOME COVER.

WE MUST BE VERY QUIET. IF THE REDCOATS CATCH US RETREATING THEY WILL CUT US TO RIBBONS. IF YOU CAN SEND MESSENGERS AND GATHER OUR SOLDIERS, MY MEN AND I WILL TAKE CARE OF EVERYTHING ELSE.
MESSENGERS FAN OUT TO SPREAD THE WORD AS WASHINGTON'S ARMY ASSEMBLES ON THE BANKS OF THE EAST RIVER, READY FOR EVACUATION.

SO ALL THROUGH THE NIGHT, IN HEAVY RAIN AND STRONG WINDS, GENERAL GLOVER'S MARBLEHEADERS REGIMENT ROWED WASHINGTON'S ARMY ACROSS THE EAST RIVER, SO THEY COULD ESCAPE TO FIGHT AGAIN ANOTHER DAY.
THEY ROWED MEN AND CANNON, HORSES AND SUPPLIES. ALL NIGHT LONG, THEY ROWED BACK AND FORTH. WHEN MORNING CAME AND THE BRITISH REACHED THE BANKS OF THE RIVER, ALL THEY FOUND WERE A FEW RUSTY BUCKETS.

JUST IN TIME.
THE BRITISH TROOPS CONTINUED TO ADVANCE, BUT WASHINGTON WAS ABLE TO OUTRUN THEM AND REGROUP. A FEW MONTHS LATER, ON CHRISTMAS NIGHT, GENERAL GLOVER AND HIS MEN ONCE AGAIN PLAYED A MAJOR ROLE IN THE WAR. THEY FERRIED WASHINGTON AND 2400 SOLDIERS ACROSS THE ICE-FILLED DELAWARE RIVER FOR A SURPRISE ATTACK ON THE BRITISH AND HESSIANS CAMPED IN TRENTON, NJ. THE ATTACK WAS A MAJOR SUCCESS.
WITHOUT YOU AND YOUR MEN, I AM AFRAID THE REVOLUTION WOULD BE OVER. THIS COUNTRY OWES YOU A DEBT OF GRATITUDE.
NOT AT ALL, SIR. WE WERE JUST DOING OUR DUTY. AS CITIZENS OF THIS NEW COUNTRY, IT IS PART OF OUR RESPONSIBILTY TO SERVE IN ANY WAY WE CAN. WHEN THIS WAR IS OVER, WE WILL RETURN TO OUR JOBS AND FAMILIES. BUT UNTIL THEN, THE MARBLEHEADERS AND I WILL ALWAYS BE READY, SIR.

UNIT 2

Creating a Nation

ORDER!
ORDER, GENTLEMEN!

THIS IS VERY IMPORTANT BUSINESS HERE. BEFORE WE BEGIN DISCUSSING THE CONSTITUTION IN MORE DETAIL, ARE THERE ANY QUESTIONS?
MR. FRANKLIN?

NONE HERE, MR. WASHINGTON. NOW, WHERE WERE WE?

MR. MADISON, COULD YOU TELL US WHERE WE LEFT OFF?

CERTAINLY... WE WERE JUST DISCUSSING THE STRUCTURE OF THE LEGISLA-TURE. MR. PAT-ERSON FROM NEW JERSEY HAD THE FLOOR.

THANK YOU, SIR.
I MUST URGE THE CONVENTION TO GIVE EACH STATE ONE VOTE IN THE LEGISLATURE. IT IS THE ONLY FAIR WAY TO...

FAIR? I'M SORRY, BUT I MUST DISAGREE. WHY SHOULD SOME SMALL STATE LIKE NEW JERSEY GET THE SAME VOICE AS MY HOME STATE OF VIRGINIA?

WE MUST BASE REPRESENTATION ON POPULATION.
EVERY STATE SHOULD BE EQUAL IN THE UNION, MR. RANDOLPH.

NOW, I'M SURE WE CAN FIND A COMMON GROUND. WHAT IF WE WERE TO HAVE A TWO-HOUSE LEGISLATURE?

THEN WE COULD HAVE A LOWER HOUSE BASED ON POPULATION AND AN UPPER HOUSE THAT GIVES EACH STATE EQUAL REPRESENTATION. WILL THAT WORK FOR YOU, MR. RANDOLPH?

I'M NOT SURE IF I LIKE THE TERM "LOWER HOUSE, MR. SHERMAN" BUT I FIND YOUR COMPROMISE SATISFACTORY.

I MIGHT EVEN CALL IT "GREAT." MOVING ALONG, LET US DISCUSS THE JUDICIARY...

AND SO YOU SEE, CLASS, OUR FOUNDING FATHERS HAD MANY ISSUES TO DISCUSS AT THE CONSTITUTIONAL CONVENTION.
THEY DID NOT ALWAYS SEE EYE-TO-EYE, SUCH AS THE ISSUE OF THE STRUCTURE OF THE LEGISLATURE, BUT COMPROMISE OFTEN FOUND A COMMON GROUND.

CAN ANYONE TELL ME WHAT OTHER ISSUES CAUSED DISAGREEMENT AT THE CONSTITUTIONAL CONVENTION?

WASN'T THERE SOME PROBLEM WITH GETTING THE CONSTITUTION OKAYED BY ALL OF THE STATES?

YEAH, DIDN'T IT TAKE, LIKE, A COUPLE OF YEARS FOR IT TO GET RATIFIED?

WHY WOULD IT TAKE SO LONG TO GET IT RATIFIED?

WELL, GETTING THE CONSTITUTION APPROVED WAS NOT AN EASY PROCESS. NINE OF THE THIRTEEN STATES IN THE UNION HAD TO APPROVE IT. ALL THIRTEEN STATES WOULD EVENTUALLY RATIFY THE CONSTITUTION BY 1790.

NOW, WE ALL KNOW WHO GEORGE WASH-INGTON IS, BUT CAN ANYONE NAME THE OTHER MEN IN THIS PAINTING?

Unit 3

Launching the Republic

George Washington (1732-99)
The name of America belongs to you in your national capacity.
I see a land that has united in a common cause.
I see the ever-favorite object of my heart...
I see a land full of life and possi-bilities...
...a place to call home.
And the happy reward of freedom around me.
The future is bright. Bright indeed.
©2005 Mark Carolan

UNIT 3

Launching the Republic

ELECTION DEADLOCK!

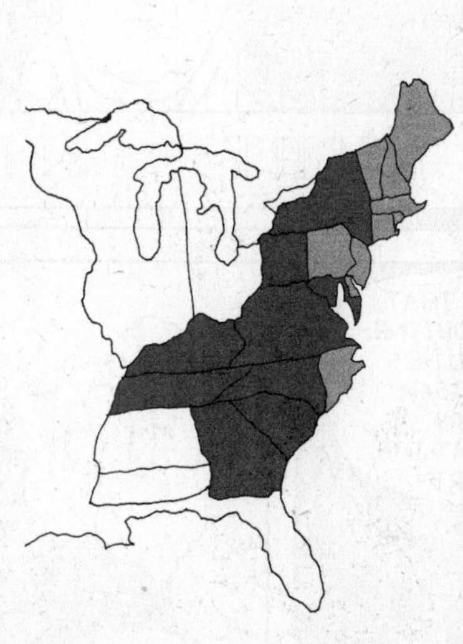

AN ANN SPECIAL REPORT

THE ELECTION OF 1800 WAS THE FIRST TRULY CONTESTED ELECTION IN U.S. HISTORY. THE CANDIDATES INCLUDED THOMAS JEFFERSON, JOHN ADAMS (THE INCUMBENT), AND AARON BURR. IN THESE EARLY DAYS OF THE ELECTORAL COLLEGE SYSTEM, THERE WEREN'T ANY PARTY "TICKETS" WITH A PRESIDENTIAL CANDIDATE AND A VICE PRESIDENTIAL CHOICE.

INSTEAD, EVERYONE RAN FOR PRESIDENT, WITH THE WINNER OF ELECTORAL VOTES EARNING THE PRESIDENTIAL OFFICE AND THE RUNNER-UP BEING AWARDED THE VICE PRESIDENCY, EVEN IF THE TWO WERE FROM OPPOSING PARTIES!

ANN
LIVE
GOOD EVENING, I'M JONATHAN WILLIAMS, AND THIS IS THE AMERICAN NEWS NETWORK, WITH BREAKING ELECTION-NIGHT COVERAGE. WELL, WE'RE JUST NOW RECEIVING THE FINAL ELECTORAL VOTE TALLIES FROM ALL 16 STATES...
AND AGAIN, THIS YEAR'S VOTE LOOKED TO BE A BATTLE BETWEEN THE TWO EMERGING POLITICAL PARTIES IN AMERICAN POLITICS: THE DEMOCRATIC-REPUBLICANS AND THE FEDERALISTS...
ELECTION NIGHT SPECIAL REPORT

OKAY, I'M RECEIVING WORD NOW THAT, WITH 68% OF THE PRECINCTS REPORTING, WE CAN PROJECT A WINNER...AND HE'S FROM THE DEMOCRATIC-REPUBLICAN PARTY! IT'S A NARROW VICTORY, APPARENTLY. LET'S HAVE A LOOK AT THE ELECTORAL COLLEGE MAP CHART.

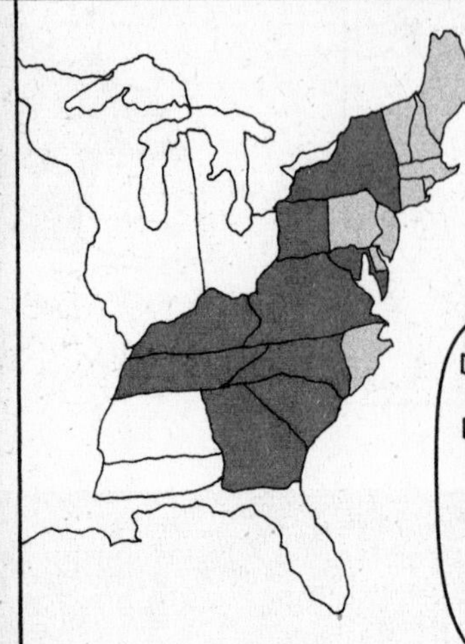

DEM-REP 73
FED 65
SO IT LOOKS LIKE THE DEMOCRATIC-REPUBLICANS, REPRESENTED HERE BY THE DARK GRAY STATES, HAVE A NARROW EDGE OF JUST 8 ELECTORAL VOTES; BY ALL APPEARANCES, THOMAS JEFFERSON WILL INDEED BE OUR THIRD PRESIDENT --WAIT, I'M GETTING ANOTHER UPDATE...

LADIES AND GENTLEMEN, I'M JUST NOW RECEIVING WORD THAT THE DEMOCRATIC-REPUBLICAN CANDIDATES HAVE RECEIVED THE SAME NUMBER OF VOTES! IT LOOKS LIKE OUR PROJECTION WAS A BIT PREMATURE!

THOMAS JEFFERSON AND AARON BURR EACH RECEIVED 73 ELECTORAL VOTES. HOW IS THIS POSSIBLE?

WHILE WE AWAIT CONFIRMATION ON THESE NUMBERS, I'M GOING TO ASK OUR POLITICAL SCIENCE EXPERT SAMUEL WILLIAMSON FOR HIS THOUGHTS ON THIS...SAMUEL, WAS THERE ANY INDICATION THIS WAS GOING TO HAPPEN AND, WELL, WHERE DO WE GO FROM HERE?

FRANKLY JONATHAN, I THINK SOMETHING LIKE THIS WAS BOUND TO OCCUR, GIVEN THE SYSTEM CURRENTLY IN PLACE.

THE DEMOCRATIC-REPUBLICAN CANDIDATES
IN A PROCESS WHERE 2 MEN CAN RUN FOR PRESIDENT **IN THE SAME PARTY**, AND WITH THE ELECTORATE HAVING 2 VOTES EACH TO SPLIT, IT'S EASY TO SEE HOW THIS COULD HAVE HAPPENED...

OKAY, SO WE HAVE A TIE BETWEEN BURR AND JEFFERSON. WHAT NOW? DO WE RECOUNT THE VOTES? DO WE HAVE COPRESIDENTS?
IF I'M NOT MISTAKEN, THE CONSTITUTION HAS A PLAN FOR JUST THIS SCENARIO...BASICALLY THE HOUSE OF REPRESENTATIVES GETS TO VOTE ON THE ULTIMATE OUTCOME.

HMM. WELL THERE YOU HAVE IT, FOLKS. THE FATE OF THE PRESIDENCY IS IN THE HANDS OF THE HOUSE OF REPRESENTATIVES. HOW LONG WILL THE DELIBERATIONS TAKE? WHATEVER HAPPENS, STAY TUNED TO ANN FOR FURTHER DEVELOPMENTS!

SIX DAYS LATER.

...TODAY MARKS DAY SIX SINCE THE HOUSE OF REPRESENTATIVES FIRST WENT INTO DELIBERATIONS TO DECIDE THE VIRTUAL TIE BETWEEN AARON BURR AND THOMAS JEFFERSON. WE'VE RECEIVED WORD THAT A TOTAL OF 35 BALLOTS HAVE BEEN CAST IN THE LAST 5 DAYS, AND STILL WITH NO CLEAR WINNER!

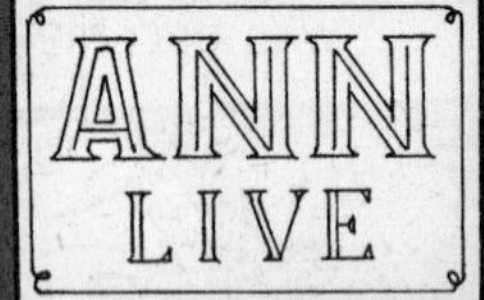

ELECTION SPECIAL REPORT

SO SAMUEL, THE QUESTION I HAVE IS THIS: WE BOTH KNOW THAT THE MAJORITY OF THE HOUSE IS MADE UP OF FEDERALISTS, WHO LOATHE THE JEFFERSON! SO WHY HAVE THEY NOT VOTED HIM OUT OF THIS RACE YET?
WELL, MY GUESS IS THAT OUR OLD FRIEND ALEXANDER HAMILTON IS THE CULPRIT HERE...WE ALL KNOW HAMILTON DOESN'T LIKE JEFFERSON, BUT HE LIKES BURR EVEN LESS!

IN MY OPINION, THOMAS JEFFERSON IS BY FAR NOT SO DANGEROUS A MAN AS AARON BURR.
ANN ALEXANDER HAMILTON

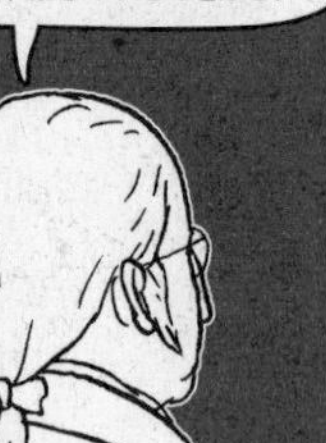

I THINK HAMILTON IS WORKING TO INFLUENCE HIS OWN FEDERALIST PARTY TO VOTE AGAINST BURR, WHICH IS JUST PROLONGING THIS PROCESS.

WE'VE ALSO BEEN HEARING RUMORS THAT JEFFERSON HIMSELF IS ASSURING THE FEDERALISTS WHO ARE OPPOSED TO HIM THAT HE WILL NOT FIRE THEM IF HE INDEED IS ELECTED.

IT DOESN'T SOUND GOOD FOR BURR. AND TO TELL YOU THE TRUTH, THIS IS THE KIND OF PARTISAN CONFLICT GEORGE WASHINGTON WARNED ABOUT IN HIS PRESIDENTIAL FAREWELL ADDRESS...

I HAVE ALREADY TOLD YOU OF THE DANGER OF PARTIES IN THE STATE, WITH PARTICULAR REFERENCE TO THE FOUNDING OF THEM ON GEOGRAPHICAL DISCRIMINATIONS...
THE DOMINATION OF ONE PARTY OVER ANOTHER, SHARPENED BY THE SPIRIT OF REVENGE, NATURAL TO PARTY DISAGREEMENT, WHICH IN DIFFERENT AGES AND COUNTRIES HAS CAUSED THE MOST HORRID PROBLEMS, IS ITSELF A FRIGHTFUL SYSTEM OF GOVERNMENT.

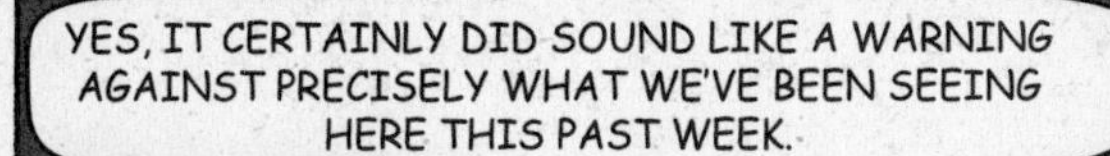

YES, IT CERTAINLY DID SOUND LIKE A WARNING AGAINST PRECISELY WHAT WE'VE BEEN SEEING HERE THIS PAST WEEK.
HMM. IT'S SOMETHING THAT COULD DEFINITELY BE DAMAGING TO THE COUNTRY IN THE FUTURE.

HOLD ON SAMUEL, I'M RECEIVING ANOTHER UPDATE...YES, IT SOUNDS LIKE YOUR PREDICTIONS WERE RIGHT! JEFFERSON HAS WON THE HOUSE OF REPRESENTATIVE'S VOTE, WITH 10 STATES TO BURR'S 4!

ANN
LIVE

YOU HEARD IT HERE FIRST, AMERICA! THOMAS JEFFERSON IS YOUR THIRD PRESIDENT. AND WORD IS CONGRESS WILL CALL FOR A CONSTITUTIONAL AMENDMENT TO PREVENT A PROBLEM LIKE THIS FROM EVER HAPPENING AGAIN...

LET'S HOPE ALL ELECTIONS IN AMERICA'S FUTURE ARE DECISIVE AND FREE OF CONTROVERSY.
THE END

Unit 3

Launching the Republic

On Her Own

MRS. STONE WILL TAKE GOOD CARE OF ME, FATHER. SHE LOOKS AFTER ALL HER MILL GIRLS, DON'T YOU, MRS. STONE?
I DO, INDEED.

ABBY'LL GET THREE GOOD MEALS A DAY. SHE'LL BE IN BY 10:00 AT NIGHT. AND I'LL MAKE SURE SHE'S TO CHURCH ON SUNDAY.

PROMISE ME YOU'LL WRITE OFTEN.
I WILL--EVERY WEEK. DON'T WORRY, FATHER!
BYE!

INSIDE THE BOARDINGHOUSE A FEW MINUTES LATER
SARAH HERE WILL HELP YOU GET SETTLED. SUPPER'S AT 7:00.
I CAN'T BELIEVE IT!

I'M REALLY IN LOWELL!

MY **OWN BED!**
IN A ROOM WITH ONLY **ONE OTHER PERSON!**

A FEW HOURS LATER
WHAT AN EVENING!
AREN'T THE SOCIALS WONDERFUL? JUST WAIT 'TIL WEDNESDAY EVENINGS.
THERE ARE LECTURES IN THE TOWN HALL ON ALL KINDS OF THINGS!

6:20 TUESDAY MORNING
HEAR THAT BELL?
IT MEANS WE BETTER GO INTO THE FACTORY.
RRRING!

THE DINNER BELL'S AT NOON--WE'LL MEET HERE, AND HEAD TO THE BOARDINGHOUSE TO EAT, THEN BACK HERE BY THE 12:35 BELL.

I'M THE OVERSEER FOR THIS SECTION. EMILY WILL SHOW YOU HOW TO USE A LOOM. SOON ENOUGH, YOU'LL BE TENDING THREE AT A TIME, LIKE HER!

MIND YOU--ALWAYS WEAR YOUR HAIR UP. THE MACHINES'LL RIP IT RIGHT OUT IF YOU GET IT CAUGHT IN THEM.
SAME GOES FOR YOUR FINGERS.

6:30 P.M.
RRRING
WHEW!

WEDNESDAY EVENING
I CAN'T BELIEVE IT--A LECTURE BY RALPH WALDO EMERSON!
WHAT AN EXPERIENCE!

THURSDAY
WHAT'S THIS?...BOTANY COURSE...GERMAN CLASS...POETRY WRITING?
WHEN ENOUGH GIRLS ARE INTERESTED IN A TOPIC, THEY FIND SOMEONE TO TEACH A COURSE. A NOTICE IS POSTED, AND ANYONE WHO WANTS TO CAN SIGN UP.
12 CLASSES FOR $1.

WE SHOULD DO IT!
I'D NEVER GET A CHANCE LIKE THIS AT HOME!

FRIDAY
WHEW! WHY IS IT ALWAYS SO HOT IN THERE?
THE MACHINES GIVE OFF A GREAT DEAL OF HEAT, AND THE WINDOWS ARE NEVER OPENED.
NO MATTER WHAT.

IN THE WINTER, THE MACHINES ARE THE ONLY THING HEATING THE FACTORY!
!

SATURDAY

WHAT HAPPENED BACK THERE?
SIGH...I'M NOT AS PRODUCTIVE AS THE OTHER GIRLS, SO I MAY LOSE MY JOB.
YOU KNOW ABOUT THE PREMIUM SYSTEM, RIGHT? AN OVERSEER GETS A BONUS FOR GETTING THE MOST WORK OUT OF HIS WORKERS.

SUNDAY
DEAR FATHER AND MOTHER,
MRS. STONE TOOK ME TO CHURCH TODAY AS PROMISED. THE MINISTER GAVE AN EXCELLENT SERMON ON THE BENEFITS OF HARD WORK. LATER SARAH AND I WENT WINDOW SHOPPING. THERE ARE SO MANY STORES HERE...
GIVE MY LOVE TO EVERYONE. I MISS YOU ALL.
YOUR OBEDIENT DAUGHTER,
ABBY WEBSTER

SIX MONTHS LATER ON A MONDAY MORNING
I DON'T BELIEVE IT!
I'LL QUIT!
WHAT'S HAPPENED?
THEY WOULDN'T DARE!
THE COMPANY'S CUTTING OUR WAGES THE FIRST OF THE MONTH.

OH, NO! WHAT CAN WE DO?

THAT EVENING
...GO HOME...
...UNFAIR...
...CAN'T AFFORD...
...STRIKE!

Dear Father and Mother,

I have so many friends here, but I miss you so much. I cannot decide whether to stay here or return home.

I have bad news about the mill. The owners have cut our pay. Many girls have gone on strike, including me...

Your loving daughter,

Abby Webster

UNIT 4

Nationalism and Sectionalism

Through treaties with the U.S. government, the Cherokee had become a sovereign nation within Georgia. As more and more American settlers began to move to nearby areas, the Cherokee's land was threatened. In an attempt to avoid being removed from their land, the Cherokee began a concentrated effort to adapt their culture to that of mainstream America.
A Cherokee named Sequoya helped begin this process by adapting the Cherokee language into an alphabet.

Many were skeptical at first . . .
. . . but Sequoya convinced his people that if they tried to adapt their culture to that of the white man, they could save their land.

Some still opposed such changes . . .
. . . but the Cherokee continued to change their community.

The Cherokee would eventually sue the state of Georgia in order to keep their status as a sovereign nation. They took their case to John Marshall and the Supreme Court and won.
President Jackson, however, had other ideas . . .
"John Marshall has made his decision. Now let him enforce it."
-Andrew Jackson

Unit 4

Nationalism and Sectionalism

From Sea to Shining Sea!

HURRY DAD! I DON'T WANT TO MISS SEEING THE PRESIDENT!

CAN YOU SEE THE PRESIDENT NOW, SON?
I SEE HIM!
TODAY WE SALUTE THOSE BRAVE AMERICANS WHO HELPED SHAPE OUR COUNTRY.
WE SALUTE THOSE WHO FOUGHT SO BRAVELY FOR INDEPENDENCE IN TEXAS, ESPECIALLY THOSE WHO DIED AT THE ALAMO.
AND IN THE WAR WITH MEXICO - WITHOUT THOSE BRAVE SOULS WE WOULD NOT HAVE ESTABLISHED NEW MEXICO!
WE SALUTE THOSE WHO TRAVELED THOUSANDS OF MILES TO REACH CALIFORNIA - DESPITE LACK OF WATER AND SHELTER FROM THE SUN.

WE SALUTE THE MORMON PIONEERS WHO ESTABLISHED SETTLEMENTS IN THE UTAH TERRITORY.

WE SALUTE THOSE WHO WORKED SO HARD FOR THE GADSDEN PURCHASE, FOR WITHOUT IT WE WOULD NOT HAVE ESTABLISHED ALL OF ARIZONA AND NEW MEXICO!

BY BRIAN RALPH

UNIT 4

Nationalism and Sectionalism

ALL ABOARD!!

BOM DIA*... THE SEAT, IS IT OPEN?
SURE! BE OUR GUEST.
* GOOD DAY

SAY, THAT'S AN INTERESTING ACCENT.
WHERE ARE YOU FROM?

OBRIGADO.* I AM FROM PORTUGAL. HERE ON BUSINESS.
* THANK YOU

PLEASED TO MEET YOU. WE'RE THE MILLERS FROM NEW YORK.
VITOR ROMÃO OF LISBON.

WE'RE GOING TO ATLANTA. VACATION. I DON'T LIKE HOW THEY TREAT THEIR PEOPLE, BUT IT SURE IS BEAUTIFUL.

IF YOU DON'T MIND MY ASKING, WHY ARE YOU HEADING SOUTH FOR BUSINESS?

I'M SEARCHING FOR INVESTMENT OPPORTUNITY.
I'VE HEARD THINGS OF RALEIGH.

YOU SHOULD TRY IN THE NORTH. THERE'S INCREDIBLE INDUSTRY.
TEXTILES
I SEE.

WE'VE GOT LUMBER, WAGONS, SHOES...

NOT TO MENTION FARMING AND AGRICULTURE!

EXCUSE ME.
I COULDN'T HELP HEARING YOUR CONVERSATION...

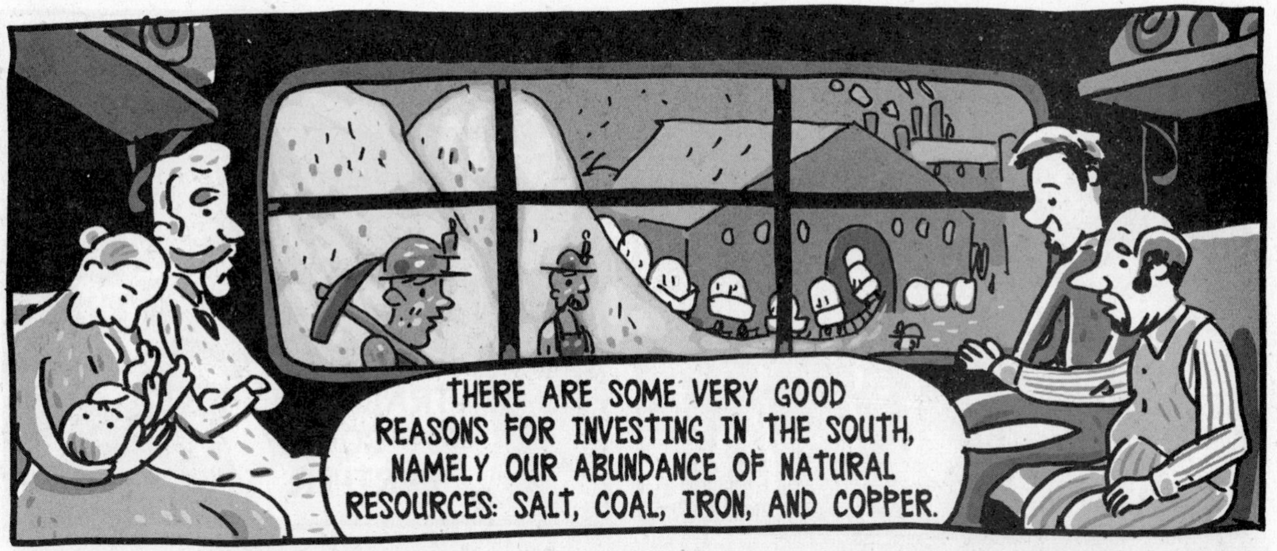
THERE ARE SOME VERY GOOD REASONS FOR INVESTING IN THE SOUTH, NAMELY OUR ABUNDANCE OF NATURAL RESOURCES: SALT, COAL, IRON, AND COPPER.

WE MIGHT NOT BE AS INDUSTRIALIZED AS THE NORTH BUT WE HAVE RAW MATERIALS.

AND OF COURSE, AS ALWAYS, COTTON IS *KING!*

YES, I'VE HEARD MUCH ABOUT THIS KING COTTON!

TIME TO GET OFF, FOLKS!

IS THIS RALEIGH?
WE RAN OUT OF TRACK.
THE TRAIN CAN NOT GO ANY FARTHER.

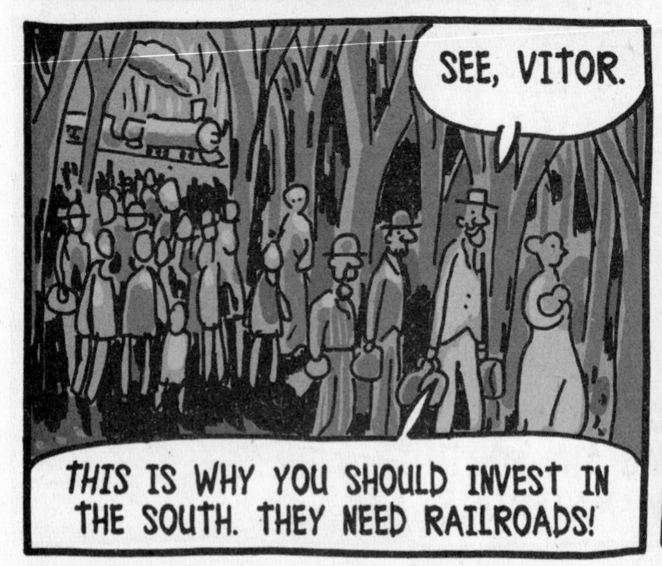
SEE, VITOR.
THIS IS WHY YOU SHOULD INVEST IN THE SOUTH. THEY NEED RAILROADS!

THIS IS WHERE I DEPART. HAVE A GOOD REST OF YOUR TRIP.
GOOD LUCK TO YOU, VITOR.
ADEUS.
GOODBYE.

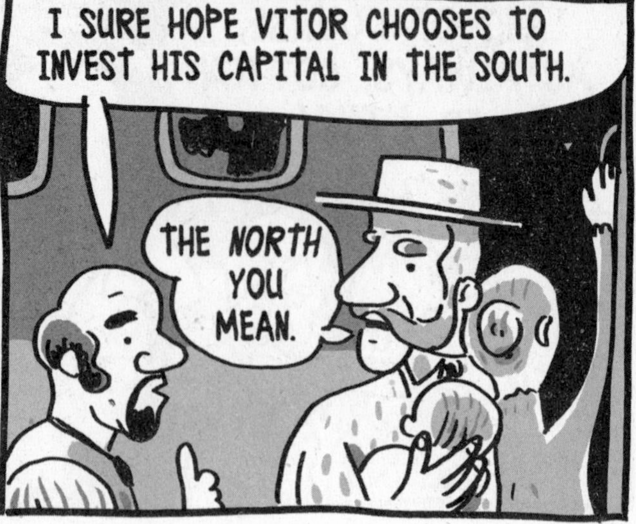
I SURE HOPE VITOR CHOOSES TO INVEST HIS CAPITAL IN THE SOUTH.
THE NORTH YOU MEAN.

I SHOULD HAVE MENTIONED OUR WORK FORCE. *THAT* WOULD HAVE CONVINCED VITOR!

Gregory Benton
The end

Unit 5

Civil War and Reconstruction

April 12th 1850. In a small town...
YES, OF COURSE.
THANK YOU, MARY.
THAT WAS A WONDERFUL SERVICE TODAY. OH, SO WHAT WERE YOU AND SARAH TALKING ABOUT?
I'M THINKING OF HELPING HER ON THE UNDERGROUND RAILROAD.
GOODNESS MARY, DON'T YOU THINK WE SHOULD TALK ABOUT THIS FIRST? IT'S EXTREMELY DANGEROUS.
I'VE HEARD SOME BAD STORIES OF WHAT GOES ON. GOOD FOLK ARE GETTING BEATEN VERY BADLY FOR HELPING ESCAPED SLAVES.
I KNOW THE DANGERS, JACK. BUT I'VE ALSO HEARD STORIES OF WHAT IS HAPPENING TO THOSE POOR CAPTIVES DOWN SOUTH. IT'S QUITE HORRIFYING AND IT MUST STOP.
Meanwhile, in a small town further South...

MARY, THE SLAVES BELONG TO THE FARMERS. WE SHOULDN'T GET INVOLVED.
BUT THAT'S MY POINT JACK. THEY ARE NOT ANIMALS. THEY SHOULDN'T BELONG TO ANYONE. THEY ARE HUMAN BEINGS JUST LIKE US.
I FEEL VERY STRONGLY ABOUT THIS. WE DON'T NEED TO DO MUCH OTHER THAN HELP THEM GET TO THE NORTH WHERE THEY'LL BE SAFE.
I DON'T KNOW MARY. I'M NOT COMFORTABLE WITH IT. WHAT DO YOU PLAN TO DO?
ALL WE NEED TO DO IS GIVE THEM A PLACE TO SLEEP AS THEY PASS THROUGH THIS WAY. OUR HOME WILL BECOME A 'SAFE HOUSE' FOR THEM.
WHERE WILL WE PUT THEM? THERE ISN'T MUCH ROOM IN THE HOUSE.
WE COULD MAKE SPACE IN THE BARN.
LET'S SLEEP ON IT AND TALK AGAIN IN THE MORNING.

Morning came and Mary set out early with Sarah in search of an escaped slave rumoured to be hiding out in the woods.
It wasn't long before they arrived there...
The rumours were correct.
Mary gently reached down...

HERE, TAKE A SEAT AND REST.
Jack arrives...
YOU'RE A VERY LUCKY MAN TO HAVE MY WIFE TAKE CARE OF YOU. NOW TAKE OFF YOUR HAT AND LET ME HAVE A LOOK AT YOU.
YES SIR, OF COURSE, SIR.
I WOULD LIKE TO THANK YOU KINDLY, BOTH YOU AND YOUR GOOD LADY WIFE FOR HELPING ME OUT, SIR. MY NAME IS MADELINE ADAMS. MADDIE FOR SHORT.
GOOD LORD...YOU'RE...YOU'RE A GIRL!
MARY! FETCH ME A HOT TOWEL! THE GOOD LORD ABOVE, WHAT HAPPENED TO YOUR FACE? HOW DID YOU GET IN SUCH A WAY?
MY MASTER DID IT TO ME. HE SAID I SHOULDN'T HAVE DROPPED THE BAG OF SEEDS. BUT MY HANDS WERE SORE, AND I COULDN'T CARRY IT ANY MORE.
That wasn't the only time the 'Master' hurt Maddie. Her hands were cut and her back displayed whip marks deep into the skin.

Mary prepared some much needed food for Maddie...
I WILL GO AND PREPARE A BED FOR YOU. PLEASE EAT.
I WILL GET SOME CLEAN CLOTHES FOR YOU.
THIS ATTIC ROOM ISN'T MUCH BUT IT'S WARM AND YOU'LL NOT BE FOUND UP HERE. YOU'RE SAFE NOW.
That night, Mary hung a lantern in the window. A secret sign that their house was a 'Safe House'.
I'M SORRY THAT I DIDN'T SUPPORT YOU FROM THE BEGINNING. FROM NOW ON, WE WILL HELP WHOMEVER WE CAN.
Maddie slept well for the first time in many years.
There are many secret words used for the Underground Railroad....
AGENT:
A PERSON WHO PLOTTED THE COURSE OF ESCAPE.
BAGGAGE:
ESCAPING SLAVES.
CONDUCTORS:
PEOPLE WHO DIRECTLY TRANSPORTED SLAVES.
DRINKING GOURD:
THE NORTH STAR.
FREEDOM LINE:
THE ROUTE OF TRAVEL FOR AN ESCAPED SLAVE.
FRENCH LEAVE:
SECRET DEPARTURE.
LOAD OF POTATOES:
A WAGON OF FUGITIVE SLAVES HIDDEN UNDER THE PRODUCE.
PATTER ROLLER:
A BOUNTY HUNTER HIRED TO CAPTURE SLAVES.
PILOT:
A PERSON SERVING AS A GUIDE FOR RUNAWAYS.
SANCTUARY:
A HIDING PLACE.
SHEPHERDS:
PEOPLE WHO ENTICE SLAVES TO ESCAPE.
STATION:
A SAFE PLACE WHERE FUGITIVES COULD BE SHELTERED.
STATION MASTER:
A PERSON IN CHARGE OF A HIDING PLACE.
The Underground Railroad started its tracks from the slave states in the South and moved to the free states in the North and into Canada.
Free states
Slave states
Railroad routes

More and more slaves risked their lives trying to escape on the Underground Railroad...
...and their task was made more difficult as they were tracked by angry farmers, slave traders, and bounty hunters.
Many were hidden in secret cart compartments, in basements and barns, and even secret rooms within a 'Station' or safe house.
But the lanterns were always there to guide them to safety.
As always, the lantern was hung in Jack and Mary's window...
...ready to help anyone on the Underground Railroad.
©2005 Mark Carolan

Unit 5

Civil War and Reconstruction

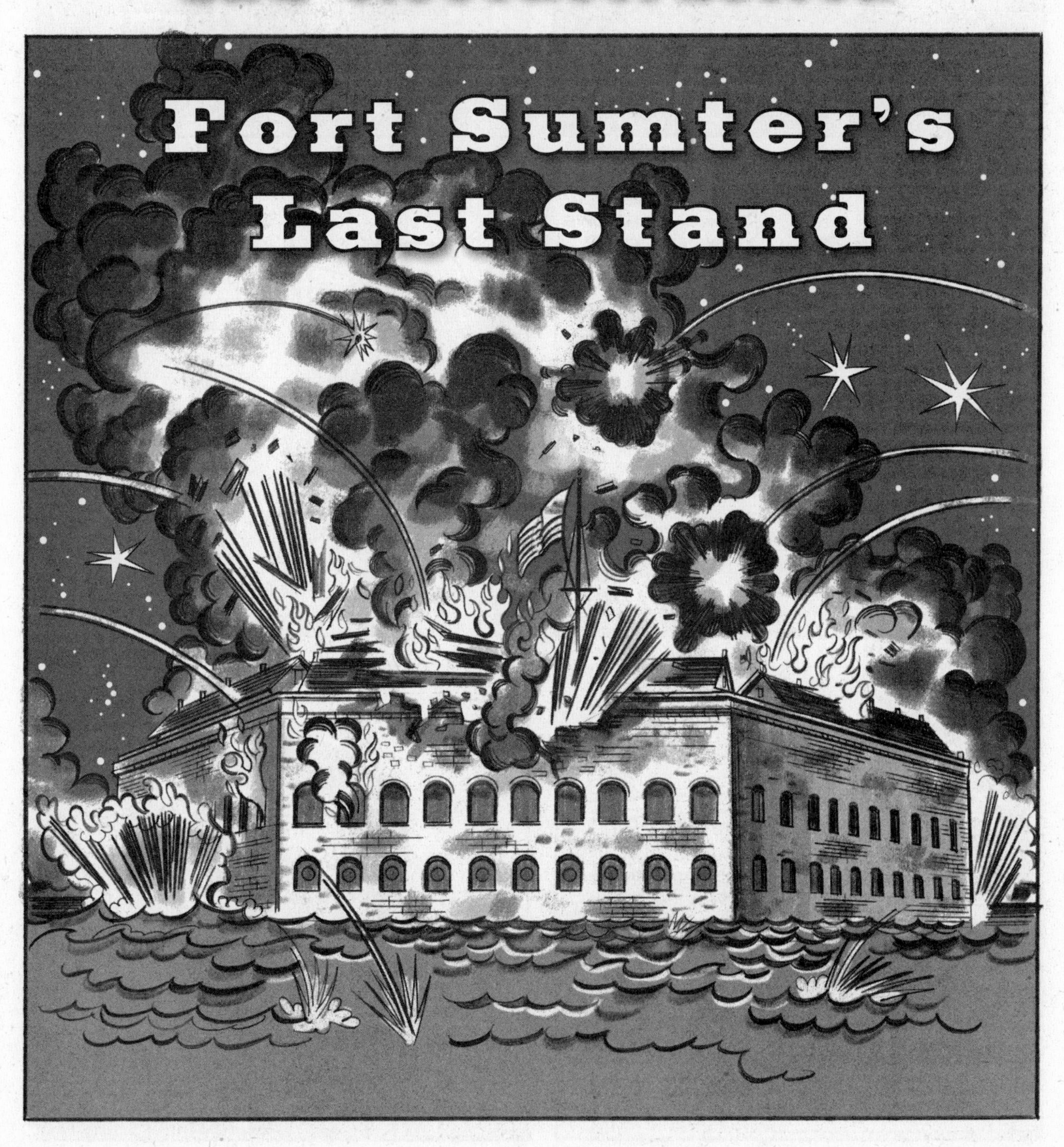

FORT SUMTER, 1861

OFFICE OF CAPTAIN CHARLES TUCKER, U.S.

IT SEEMS AS THOUGH WE MAY COME IN HARM'S WAY SOONER THAN I ANTICIPATED.

THE MEN ARE ON EDGE, BUT MAJOR ANDERSON SEEMS CONFIDENT.

SIX DAYS AFTER SOUTH CAROLINA SECEDED, WE MOVED TO OUR POSITION AT FT. SUMTER.

SOUTH CAROLINA SECESSION RALLY
DEC. 20, 1860

WE MUST STAND OUR GROUND AND UPHOLD THE UNION AT ALL COST.

THERE HAS BEEN TALK OF COMPROMISE.

SEN. JOHN CRITTENDEN HAS PROPOSED THAT LINCOLN ALLOW THE SOUTH TO KEEP SLAVERY. . .

...INCLUDING ANY NEWLY FORMED SOUTHERN STATES.

THIS MUST NOT BE ALLOWED TO HAPPEN.

PRESIDENT LINCOLN'S INAUGURATION
MARCH 4, 1861

THANKFULLY OUR NEW PRESIDENT OPPOSES THIS IDEA.

WE HAVE ONLY A FEW WEEKS
OF SUPPLIES LEFT.

MAJOR ANDERSON HAS REQUESTED A SUPPLY SHIP, BUT IT MAY NOT GET THROUGH.

OFFICE OF CONFEDERATE
PRESIDENT JEFFERSON DAVIS

THIS MUST BE STOPPED!

TO: GEN. P.G.T BEAUREGARD
FROM: PRES. JEFFERSON DAVIS
REMOVE UNION PRESENCE IN
CHARLESTON HARBOR AT ALL
COST.

FORT SUMTER: APRIL 12, 1861

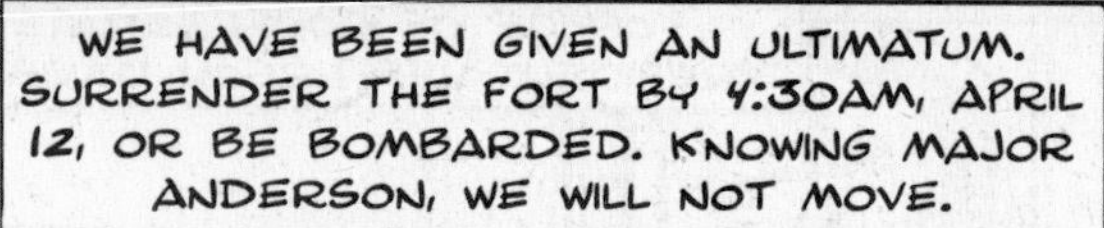
WE HAVE BEEN GIVEN AN ULTIMATUM. SURRENDER THE FORT BY 4:30AM, APRIL 12, OR BE BOMBARDED. KNOWING MAJOR ANDERSON, WE WILL NOT MOVE.

MAJOR ROBERT ANDERSON
GENTLEMEN, THE HOUR IS UPON US.

TRY NOT TO WORRY. LOVE, CHARLES

UNIT 5

Civil War and Reconstruction

THE IMPEACHMENT OF ANDREW JOHNSON

THE CIVIL WAR IS BARELY OVER, AND HE'S LETTING CONFEDERATE STATES BACK INTO THE UNION AS IF NOTHING HAPPENED.

HE VETOES ANY BILL THAT WOULD GRANT BASIC CIVIL RIGHTS TO FORMER SLAVES.

ACCORDING TO THE "*TENURE OF OFFICE ACT*", THE PRESIDENT NEEDS SENATE APPROVAL TO REPLACE CERTAIN GOVERNMENT OFFICIALS...

...BUT DID JOHNSON ***GET*** SENATE APPROVAL WHEN HE KICKED OUT SECRETARY OF WAR EDWIN STANTON?

THIS MESSAGE BROUGHT TO YOU BY THE RADICAL REPUBLICANS OF THE UNITED STATES CONGRESS

WE'RE BACK WITH LIVE COVERAGE OF THE IMPEACHMENT TRIAL OF PRESIDENT ANDREW JOHNSON.
IN CASE YOU'RE JUST TUNING IN, LET ME RECAP THE EVENTS OF THE PAST FEW MONTHS.
COURT NEWS

FOLLOWING THE CIVIL WAR AND LINCOLN'S ASSASSINATION, THE REPUBLICANS IN BOTH HOUSES OF CONGRESS HAVE CLASHED OFTEN WITH THE PRESIDENT, A DEMOCRAT.

AGAIN AND AGAIN, CONGRESS HAS OVERRIDDEN JOHNSON'S VETOES, PASSING LAWS THAT HE BELIEVES TO BE UNJUST OR UNCONSTITUTIONAL.
VETO

BOOT!
THE FINAL STRAW, HOWEVER, CAME WHEN JOHNSON VIOLATED THE 1867 TENURE OF OFFICE ACT, WHICH HAD BANNED THE PRESIDENT FROM REMOVING GOVERNMENT OFFICIALS.

IS THIS A TRUE BATTLE OF IDEALS, OR ARE BOTH PARTIES SIMPLY TRYING TO HOLD ON TO THEIR POWER?
NO ONE KNOWS FOR SURE.

THIS FEBRUARY, THE HOUSE VOTED 124 TO 47 IN FAVOR OF IMPEACHING THE PRESIDENT.
IF HE'S BEEN IMPEACHED, WHY IS HE STILL IN OFFICE? WHY ARE WE HERE? LET'S ASK OUR POLITICAL ANALYST.

"IMPEACHMENT" REFERS NOT TO THE ACT OF REMOVING ONE FROM OFFICE, BUT RATHER TO THE FORMAL ACCUSATION OF WRONGDOING, LEADING TO A TRIAL BEFORE THE SENATE.
MURRAY McANDREW
Political Analyst

ONLY IF JOHNSON IS FOUND GUILTY OF THE ARTICLES OF IMPEACHMENT WILL HE BE REQUIRED TO LEAVE OFFICE.

FASCINATING STUFF. SUPPORTERS OF THE PRESIDENT ARE GATHERED OUTSIDE TODAY.
LET'S SEE WHAT THEY HAVE TO SAY.
I GET IT--WE WON THE CIVIL WAR, BUT THE REPUBLICANS WANT TO TREAT THE SOUTH LIKE A CONQUERED LAND, MAKING UP NEW RULES AND NEW BORDERS.
GO ANDY

ALL JOHNSON IS DOING IS TRYING TO SPEED THINGS ALONG BY ALLOWING THE OLD STATES BACK IN THE UNION WITH THEIR OLD LAWS INTACT.
IS KINDNESS A CRIME?

MAYBE NOT, BUT THOSE "OLD LAWS" DON'T ALLOW BLACK CITIZENS THE RIGHT TO VOTE. WHAT ABOUT THE TENURE OF OFFICE ACT? HE BROKE THE LAW!

THIRTY-SIX VOTES ARE NEEDED TO REMOVE JOHNSON FROM OFFICE. THIRTY-FIVE ARE NEARLY CERTAIN, WITH THE CRITICAL VOTE COMING DOWN TO KANSAS SENATOR EDMUND ROSS.

C'MON...
C'MON...

YES?

NOT GUILTY.

WOO HOO!

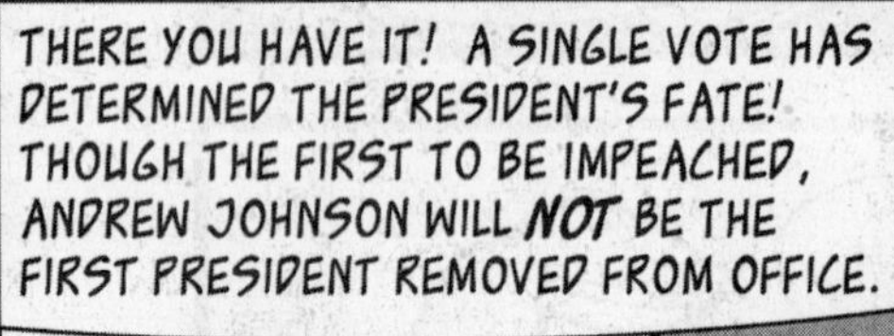
THERE YOU HAVE IT! A SINGLE VOTE HAS DETERMINED THE PRESIDENT'S FATE! THOUGH THE FIRST TO BE IMPEACHED, ANDREW JOHNSON WILL *NOT* BE THE FIRST PRESIDENT REMOVED FROM OFFICE.

HE WILL REMAIN IN POWER

...AT LEAST, UNTIL THE *PEOPLE* MAKE THAT DECISION IN THIS NOVEMBER'S ELECTION.
THAT'S ALL FOR NOW!